Rough Diamonds

ROUGH DIAMONDS

The Butler & Wilson Collection

Vivienne Becker

Foreword by Ali MacGraw

TO PAOLO FROM VIVIENNE

AUTHORS' ACKNOWLEDGEMENTS

This book has given me a very welcome and enjoyable opportunity to work with Nicky Butler and Simon Wilson whom I remember well as stars of the antique jewellery business when I first began to work in the trade. They both have endless and enviable energy and enthusiasm.

I would like to thank Suzy Menkes, Caroline Baker, Grace Coddington, Vanessa de Lisle, Catherine Deneuve, Sue Lawley; and Madame Denise Arnal, and Mr Biackiewicz for sharing their ideas about costume jewellery.

Thank you also to Noreen Hind at Butler & Wilson for picture research and to Jane Price for patient organisation, to Andrew Hewson, to Linda Sonntag and Bernard Higton, to my family and to all my friends for their much-valued support and encouragement, to Colin Webb, Louise Simpson and Tim Rice of Pavilion Books.

Butler & Wilson would especially like to thank Madame Denise Arnal, Mr Miczyslaw Biackiewicz, Anna Zgorska, Federico and Ellen Jimenez, Ray Petrie, Lydie, Jean-Claude, Max, Trevor and Ernesto for their encouragement and inspiration.

First published in Great Britain in 1990 by
PAVILION BOOKS LIMITED
196 Shaftesbury Avenue, London WC2H 8JL

Text copyright © Vivienne Becker 1990
Photographs copyright © Butler & Wilson 1990
unless otherwise credited in the Photographers
Acknowledgements page 175.

Designed by Bernard Higton

All rights reserved. No part of this publication may be reproduced, stored in a retrieval system, or transmitted, in any form or by any means, electronic, mechanical, photocopying, recording or otherwise, without the prior permission of the copyright holder.

A CIP catalogue record for this book is available from the British Library

ISBN 1 85145 521 3

10 9 8 7 6 5 4 3 2

Printed in Spain

CONTENTS

Foreword by Ali MacGraw 7

Introduction 8

Part One   THE JEWELS 15

     Art Nouveau 16

     Art Deco 25

     The Cocktail Jewels 41

     Butler & Wilson Revivals 46

     Butler & Wilson Originals 81

Part Two   CREATING THE IMAGE 121

     The Billboards 1982-1990 134

     The Billboard Models and Photographers 174

     Photography Acknowledgements 175

FOREWORD

A few years ago, when I was celebrating Thanksgiving, the festivities were interrupted by a large Malibu beach lizard, which climbed over the wall to confront my own Butler & Wilson lizard pinned to the fireplace. The beach lizard's eyes spiralled back into his head in wonderment as he came face to face with this twinkling, dazzling cousin. Terrified, he beat a hasty retreat, leaving my precious pet to glitter and swing its articulated rhinestone tail.

This event captures the wondrous fantasy of Butler & Wilson creations – the whimsy, dazzle and style that sets them apart from what used to be called 'plain costume jewellery'. For me, their paste rubies and *faux* pearls are far too precious to be hidden away in a drawer. Yet as traffic-stopping and glitzy as some of the pieces are, they are also classics which have redefined the whole concept of jewellery. Butler and Wilson have made it fun and exhilarating to wear fake jewels, which can look equally at home on a beautiful dress as on a denim jacket. And thanks to Nicky Butler and Simon Wilson, whom I regard not only as my friends but as inspired artists, these jewels will go on looking terrific for years to come. Like my diamond dream lizard swinging in the firelight.

Ali MacGraw

INTRODUCTION

In the last twenty-one years, costume jewellery has undergone a major transformation from déclassé substitutes for the real thing to high-profile, high-fashion creations flaunted by some of the most famous, beautiful and wealthy women in the world. Costume jewellery became the fashion phenomenon of the 1980s, the most essential accessory of the decade.

The two British designers Butler and Wilson have been largely responsible for this coming-of-age of costume jewellery. Not only did they design exciting, witty and frankly fake jewels that were more closely linked to fashion than ever before, but they also sold with them a new image of glamorous but intelligent femininity.

Nicky Butler and Simon Wilson began as antique dealers in the late 1960s, selling Art Nouveau and Art Deco jewellery, not precious but highly decorative pieces, brimming with the style and mood of their age. They had come to the antiques business at a time when the trade was opening up and attracting instinctive dealers from many different worlds and different layers of society. Antiques markets around London were full of superb undiscovered objects and larger-than-life, eccentric characters. It was an 'alternative' business at the time, quirky, intriguing and unconventional: the major work of buying was done by torchlight in the dawn gloom of the street markets of Bermondsey, Camden Passage and Portobello Road. On every corner dealers turned out their pockets to barter with other dealers over some wonderful treasure or other. There was a huge amount of new goods available every week, and stock changed hands rapidly. Butler and Wilson thrived in this atmosphere; they soon became well known for their sure taste and discriminating eye, and for their hard work in ceaselessly searching out Art Nouveau and Art Deco jewels.

The nineteenth- and twentieth-century decorative or so-called applied arts, including objects and jewellery from the 1880s to the 1930s, were being discovered in the late 1960s. It now emerged that esoteric objects reviled for so long by conventional antique dealers represented a huge potential collecting field. London salerooms held the first auctions of late Victorian and Edwardian objects, Art Nouveau and Art Deco. The organic softness and nostalgia of Art Nouveau echoed the spirit of the hippy movement and the hippy way of dress in the sixties, but by the early seventies, when fashion became more streamlined, Art Deco was seen as the epitome of style. In 1967 the enormously popular film *Bonnie and Clyde* focused attention on the clothes and atmosphere of the Jazz Age: the '20s and '30s.

Butler and Wilson took their own stall in various markets, first in Portobello Road in 1968, then in the Chelsea Antiques Market in 1969, constantly expanding and improving their stock. When Antiquarius, the huge and fashionable indoor market opened in Kings Road, Chelsea in 1970, Butler and Wilson took their first permanent stand, which soon became a cult shopping spot for the famous and the fashion-conscious. Looking for a new style to suit a new decade, customers were seeking out exciting, alternative accessories to express their individuality.

Butler and Wilson's tiny cramped but charismatic stand also attracted attention from the new influential fashion editors of the time, in particular Caroline Baker on *Nova* and Grace Coddington on *Vogue*. They both loved the gentle but rich period jewels that contributed so much character to their milestone fashion shots. Grace Coddington says: 'I was never a jewellery person. Butler and Wilson introduced me to jewellery and after that I could never do a fashion shot without masses of their period pieces. Butler and Wilson are influenced by the past, but now they are putting themselves and their own endless ideas into their designs.'

Caroline Baker first came across Butler and Wilson in Antiquarius, at a time when the brilliant and avant-garde magazine *Nova* was pushing towards an entirely new approach to fashion styling. Caroline Baker recalls: 'The end of the 1960s was a very creative time. In fashion we were rebelling against the established look which was either hippy or status quo. *Nova* demanded that we were outrageous; that our fashion pages were quite different from anything else at the time. We probably never took jewellery seriously until Butler and Wilson came along.'

In the late 1960s everyone was interested in form, colour, shape and style. Butler and Wilson's jewellery, graphic, and beautifully designed, inspired several of the most stunning fashion pages during *Nova*'s sadly brief career: a close-up of a plastic bug brooch on a barely covered breast, or, as a play on words, on a man's trouser 'flies'; and a sensual, up-to-date vision of the legendary Nancy Cunard, a lounging model wearing armfuls of ivory bangles, recalling the socialite's famous collection of African ivory fighting bangles.

Fashion editors at that time had immense power over their readers.

In the late 1960s Butler & Wilson jewellery contributed to *Nova*'s milestone fashion pages. The plastic cicada based on a 1930s design perfectly suited this graphic composition styled by Caroline Baker.

Introduction

The display of Pierrot jewels and objects in Butler and Wilson's 21st anniversary exhibition at Harrods in 1989.

Successful fashion editorials established a 'look' which they followed exactly. When Butler & Wilson jewels appeared, seductively presented, in *Nova* or *Vogue*, as an essential part of this look, customers rushed to Antiquarius to buy the featured pieces. But by the time the magazines appeared several months after the photographic session, the one-off jewels had always gone and Butler and Wilson quickly realized that there was a potential market for modern versions of old jewels, to appeal not to classic collectors but to the fashion-conscious concerned with the here and now.

They began to copy little brooches in silver and enamel, and at the same time to adapt or rework old elements into new jewellery, belts or choker necklaces. The business became more and more fashion-orientated. In November 1970 the *Evening Standard* wrote of 'genuine new antique links with the past. . . . Antique accessories are in so much demand that they are being made new.'

Business thrived and in 1972 they moved to a small shop in Fulham Road. With Art Deco mania raging, fuelled by Biba's peach-mirrored interiors, the Butler & Wilson shop became a mecca for Deco addicts. In July 1974 *Cosmopolitan* called them 'The Deco Duo'. Gradually they added to their stock of antiques and originals with more and more of their own designs, almost always inspired by the past but totally in tune with current trends. The shop was unique, the *New York Times* once likened it to a planetarium. Butler and Wilson concentrated on good presentation, on an open, approachable display to help customers try new ideas, new styles which they would not otherwise have considered.

The shop window has always been an important vehicle for their new image of costume jewellery. Favourite display themes have ranged from an endearing family of teddy bears, through sparkling giant spiders' webs, to a steely scenario of dustbins and shapely legs climbing ladders. Butler and Wilson have never lost their eye, and in 1985 they won the *Evening Standard*'s Display Competition with a window entirely blacked out to resemble the interior of a photographic studio. Display designer Nick Grossmark wrapped black towels on black mannequins, scattered them with sparkling jewels and then threw polaroid snaps of other jewellery on to the black floor.

Perhaps even more important than their visual sense is Butler and Wilson's understanding of the importance of personal ornamentation to women. In the 1970s, an era of feminism that translated into fashion as power dressing and the executive look, there was little room for conventional jewellery. In an effort to be accepted as equals, particularly in the office and the boardroom, women felt forced to banish traditional outward signs of femininity that might be suggestive of frivolity, weakness or subservience. Jewels, the age-old, universal symbols of luxury, beauty and femininity, suffered badly, and the 1970s became one of the least ornamented decades this century, or perhaps for several centuries. Real jewellery was diminished to the most severe, most tailored of gold chains, or single-stone diamond studs, trophies of financial achievement. Conventional costume jewellery was regarded as déclassé, and a sign that the wearer had neither the taste nor the money for the real thing.

But the primal urge towards self-decoration could not be eradicated and Butler and Wilson fixed on aspects of the female character that conventional jewellers so often denied: in particular a strident, sexual, almost savage sense of personal identity. Influenced by anything from American Indian ornaments to Scottish regalia, they often presented jewels as ritualistic or tribal emblems.

Fashion evolves as a series of reactions to what has gone before, and the 1980s exploded into a magnificent era of sparkling self-adornment. Femininity broke through its decade of repression with renewed vigour. There was a dramatic upsurge of glamour and escapism, encouraged by the *Dallas* and *Dynasty* syndrome of tough, determined but ultra-feminine women. Clothes became figure-hugging after the unstructured, layered look, and the plain fabrics and endless matt black that superseded the patterns and prints of the seventies provided the perfect backdrop for glittering jewels.

Glamour is larger than life, and with it the obsession with outrageously fake, fabulously flippant costume jewellery returned. Freed from the need to be a symbol of wealth and status, jewellery took back some of its primeval ritualistic character; jewels were there to be noticed, they played an essential role in the mating game, and therefore in social survival.

Butler and Wilson played a central role in this turnaround of attitudes in the early 1980s, and what enabled them to stay at the top was their understanding and deep appreciation of the long tradition of fine jewellery design. They did not create outrageously new ideas for the sake of it; they applied their originality within a framework of historical and twentieth-century traditions, all the time watching and anticipating current fashions. By developing an ingenious mixture of classic glamour and modern verve, they set the scene, in London, for the costume jewellery phenomenon.

The Princess of Wales wearing a Butler & Wilson jewelled decoration for a formal evening engagement.

*I*NTRODUCTION

In 1982 they expanded their premises by taking the shop next door in Fulham Road. The old shop was devoted mainly to men, selling crocodile accessories, wallets and suitcases, pens, cufflinks, flasks, old watches, and ivory dressing accessories; while the new shop, exquisitely decorated in charcoal grey and black with satinwood and glass cabinets, was stocked with a tantalizing array of jewels.

Soon after this expansion journalists began to spot the rising costume jewellery mania. In 1983 Liz Smith, then fashion editor of the *Evening Standard*, advised: 'Lock up your diamonds; stash away your pure gold chains and hoops. Forget all those quiet little touches of 18-carat class. Stylish investors are sinking their money these days into solid steel.' She was predicting Butler & Wilson's 'heavy metal' trend of 1983/4, which moved costume jewellery an important step further away from the imitative into the realm of the frankly and unashamedly 'genuine' fake.

Nineteen eighty-two saw the launch of the famous billboard posters. Catherine Deneuve was the first of an illustrious series of famous and beautiful women (and some men) who were photographed wearing Butler & Wilson jewellery by the world's top photographers. This gave the jewellery an added air of *cachet*, glamour and luxury. The cleverly conceived images captured many of the most important fashions and faces of the 1980s and at the same time charted the metamorphosis of

The interior of the South Molton Street shop continues the theme of stylish luxury established in Fulham Road using satinwood display cabinets.

costume jewellery and of the emerging post-feminist woman.

From this time Butler and Wilson led the way worldwide in fantasy jewels. Perhaps it is partly due to the versatility offered by their jewellery that fashion in the 1980s became more individual than ever. As Caroline Baker explained: 'Fashion is now so basic; the only thing that changes the look is jewellery. Women will never be dictated to the way we were in the past. So much information is thrown at us all the time, we can make our own choices. We have entered an era of complete individualism. I can't imagine it will go back.'

Vanessa de Lisle, executive editor, British *Vogue*, agrees that attitudes have changed completely in the last twenty years. 'Today everyone can wear costume jewellery to any occasion, but it has to be worn in the right way to make a distinct statement about the wearer. Butler and Wilson have always had an unerring instinct in this respect. In fashion photography big, bold jewellery is needed to make an impact and create a good picture. I think many fashion editors owe a great deal to Butler and Wilson's inspiration.'

A vision of the emerging post-feminist woman of the 1980s. Sophisticated glamour mixed with fantasy and escapism.

Suzy Menkes, fashion editor of the *Herald Tribune*, has watched closely as Butler and Wilson metamorphosed from antique dealers to fashion jewellers: 'Good fashion jewellery has to be like fashion itself: with acute antennae to changing trends and always ahead of the game. The way in which Butler and Wilson moved effortlessly from selling Art Deco collectors' items to creating a *Dynasty* world of sparkling jewels makes them leaders in the field.'

In the creative climate of the 1980s, Butler and Wilson expanded their business, opening a second shop in London in South Molton Street in 1985 and taking Butler & Wilson into major department stores in Britain and the United States. In 1988 they opened two new shops, one in Los Angeles, one in Glasgow. All over the world they were selling dreams and escapism, encouraging a highly sophisticated, highly enjoyable form of dressing-up, and bringing much-needed fun and fantasy to fashion.

Part One

THE JEWELS

Butler and Wilson's personal collection of nineteenth- and twentieth-century jewellery reflects the development of their own tastes from the art and idealism of Arts and Crafts to the high glamour of Hollywood style costume jewels of the 1940s. From their early days as antique dealers in the late 1960s and through the 1970s and '80s, they have kept some of their favourite jewels and accessories, both precious and non-precious, for their own collection, and many of these jewels have served as major inspirations for the Butler & Wilson originals. Very much a personal and subjective selection, the collection represents the purest and strongest examples of the major styles they admire, from Victorian Scottish jewellery, through Edwardian French jet to 1930s Mexican jewels, and also marks out some of the most fascinating stages in jewellery design. The collection can be seen as the springboard from which Butler and Wilson have projected their own very individual jewellery into the modern age.

Left: Art Deco pendant of matt frosted rock crystal, the simple geometric plaque of strong modernist design, the central amethyst framed with marcasite and blue-green amazonite, set in silver, c.1925-30.

Above: At the end of 1980s massive figurative diamanté gave way to rich, baroque gilt and pearl jewels.

ART NOUVEAU

Since the decline of Art Nouveau after the first decade of the century, objects and artefacts in this distinctive curvaceously decorative style had lain despised and ridiculed in dusty attics, until seen with fresh eyes in the 1960s by a new generation of dealers and collectors led by Butler and Wilson. They were attracted by the low price of Art Nouveau objects and their availability, as well as by their eccentric, strong style that conveyed the powerful spirit of its age: nostalgic, decadent and romantic and perfectly suited to the retrospective mood of the late '60s and early '70s.

The shiny, space-age newness worshipped in the early 1960s gave way to a faded, flowery nostalgia, a style with a conscience, and with this came a fresh interest in previous art-revolutions, in the youth cults of a hundred years before. Prejudices about antiques began to be swept away. Before the 1960s, any teaching of the history of art, which was usually confined to painting, and any serious study of antiques, stopped at 1860. Art Nouveau and Victoriana were considered kitsch: in extremely bad taste and with no decorative value whatsoever.

Butler and Wilson were among those who delved into the artistic eccentricities of the late nineteenth century, sensing their relevance to the 1960s and '70s. More than most, they were responsible for popularizing antique jewellery, for bringing the past into the present.

Art Nouveau was an artistic revolution, aimed very simply at taking art off exclusive 'salon' walls and bringing it into everyday life. Everyday objects and the degraded minor arts were elevated for the enjoyment of everyone. Although it had its roots in England, in the Arts and Crafts movement, Art Nouveau was primarily a French obsession and the style was at its purest in the hands of French designers.

As part of this revolution, the Art Nouveau movement created fashionable jewels in tune with the artistic mood of the moment. They were produced in quantity from humble materials and at reasonable prices, so that they would be available to a public wider than the usual wealthy jewellery-buying elite. The intrinsic value of the materials was by now regarded as far less important than the artistic content of the jewel. Designers and craftsmen, freed from the limitations of precious

The revival of interest in Art Nouveau jewellery was part of the cultural revolution of the late 1960s: in this *Vogue* photograph an Art Nouveau inspired brooch decorates a knitted cloche hat with matching cowl-necked sweater.

Right: Group of Art Nouveau horn pendants by Bonté: the horn carved and coloured to create ethereal Art Nouveau images of insects and flowers, c.1900.

stones and metals, worked in a variety of materials, concentrating on the forceful themes of Art Nouveau: world-weary plants and flowers, recalling the cycle of birth, death and rebirth; sinuous, free-flowing lines like waves of energy; writhing semi-clothed female figures, struggling towards freedom; anthropomorphic creatures, half-female, half-insect; and dreamy insects symbolizing the theme of metamorphosis as one century turned into the next.

With the turn of the century, and the metamorphosis in the arts, women were changing dramatically, moving towards emancipation and fighting to be free of nineteenth-century restrictions. It was appropriate that their jewels, the most feminine and personal of the decorative arts, should also be transformed by this striving art movement. The cult of femininity ruled the *fin de siècle*; the Belle Epoque was an intensely feminine period, with social life dominated by luscious and famous females, singers, actresses and courtesans.

Popular Art Nouveau jewels were in a sense the precursors of twentieth-century costume jewels, and they expressed all the poetic, symbolic ideals of the movement within a decorative package that was entirely new, fashionable and suited to the modern woman.

Horn, humble bull horn, was one of the most popular materials for the new style of artistic fashion jewellery. A material with qualities like those of plastic, horn was a forerunner of bakelite and celluloid, which would also be used for high fashion accessories. Horn had been used for small luxurious personal accessories such as haircombs in the seventeenth and eighteenth centuries, but it was really in the 1890s, with the onset of Art Nouveau, that the mysterious semi-translucent material was first used for jewellery.

At first, in an unprecedented move against the tyranny of the diamond over jewellery design, the mundane, valueless horn was incorporated into the most luxurious Art Nouveau creations, mixed with gold and precious gems, by the great master jewellers. Within a few years the material was adopted by inventive designers and craftsmen for use in smaller, less expensive highly decorative pendants, brooches, and hair ornaments, which were among the most popular fashion accessories of the day.

René Lalique, the genius of Art Nouveau jewellery and leader of the whole movement, is credited with the introduction of horn to fine jewellery. Lalique had bought a large white horn at the local abattoir and was fascinated by its lightness, its misty translucency, its shifting clouds of colour. He kept the horn in front of him, next to his worktable, while he reflected on how to make the best use of its strange beauty.

Horn is a difficult, intransigent material to work, and it presented Lalique with various problems. However, by 1897, he had fashioned a spectacular range of horn jewels and haircombs, transforming the tough, brittle substance into magical soft wilting flowers, leaves and insects, alive with movement and light. Lalique, together with a fellow goldsmith, Lucien Gaillard, instigated a method of patinating or coating horn using various acids, to give it a pearly bloom almost like an organic skin or sheen, a technique that was emulated to great effect on the less expensive horn pendants.

The bull horn was cut into sections and then heated and rolled out to form plaques on to which a design was traced and then cut out with a saw. The next stage was to soak the horn in hydrogen peroxide for a day, a process that gave the material its characteristic translucent quality. After this the rough edges were smoothed and polished and then while the horn was still pliable it was dipped in various chemicals to obtain the special pearly white or beige bloom. Other colours or stainings were added using dyes. The horn was then polished again and any final details, such as the wing veinings of insects, were inked in.

Art Nouveau horn brooch showing the careful colouring and patination that gave the impression of a pearly organic bloom, c.1900.

The Butler & Wilson collection includes a choice group of popular Art Nouveau horn pendants, mostly signed, and created around the most emotive of Art Nouveau designs and themes: plants, flowers, bees, and dragonflies. These jewels are the ancestors of today's costume jewellery. Although they were produced in reasonably large numbers, it is rare to find two exactly alike as they were individually made by hand. One of the features of Art Nouveau jewellery that particularly attracts and interests collectors is the fact that most designers and manufacturers signed their work, and the names most commonly found on horn jewellery are those of Bonté and GIP.

In the late 1960s Nicky Butler searched out a large and fine collection of pieces by Bonté. At the time, horn jewels were plentiful in markets in London and Paris and it was through a dealer in the Flea Market in Paris, who was selling some pendants belonging to Bonté's grandson, that Nicky Butler was introduced to the family of Bonté and came to understand how the pieces were conceived and made.

Elizabeth Bonté was a young French designer who had studied at the Ecole des Arts Décoratifs in Paris and she experimented, not too successfully, with a wide variety of unusual materials until she hit upon horn. The challenge and rewards of the material clearly appealed to her, and she produced a large range of sophisticated and beautiful brooches and pendants of carved and moulded horn, coloured, stained and patinated and hung on silk decorated with glass beads of soft, muted colours. Many of the techniques that she and her colleagues evolved for working horn are virtually lost today. Her main rival was Georges Pierre, known by his initials, GIP. Eventually, they decided to join forces and workshops and continued working together until 1936, all the time producing pretty and popular pendants in the Art Nouveau manner, until plastics took over from the natural material and the art of horn working disappeared.

Dragonflies, cicadas and other insects became important motifs in Butler and Wilson's originals in the 1980s. For a brief period in the 1970s, they commissioned new carved horn brooches, designed in the Art Nouveau spirit, and made in the Jura region in France, all hand carved and coloured.

The Art Nouveau enamels in the collection, mainly pendants and buckles, also demonstrate the turn-of-the-century move towards highly decorative, artistic jewels of low intrinsic value. The art of enamelling had been explored and perfected by French craftsmen during the nineteenth century. The goldsmith and jeweller Lucien Falize, captivated by Japanese works of art, had introduced a distinctive style of brightly coloured cloisonné enamel to his gold jewellery, while Charles Riffault, who worked for Boucheron during the 1860s, is thought to have been one of the first to revive the technique of *plique à jour*, or translucent unbacked enamel, which was to reach a high point of beauty and achievement in Art Nouveau jewellery at the turn of the century.

By 1900, fine enamels were also applied to bronze and base metal jewellery by Parisian craftsmen like Piel Frères who aimed at creating 'art jewels' for more modest budgets: an innovation greeted with much praise by contemporary art journals, who admired the quality of design and execution and its relevance to modern life. These art jewels, many of them belt buckles, and therefore very closely linked to fashion, were readily available on market stalls in the late 1960s. Butler and Wilson, attracted by their strong vibrant colours and expressive Belle Epoque designs, bought them whenever they could. They were yet unaware, however, that these items were the forerunners of twentieth-century fashion jewels, exciting modern designs executed with skill and artistry in inexpensive materials.

Silver and gilt cicada brooch recreated by Butler and Wilson after a nineteenth-century Japanese model.

One example in the Butler & Wilson collection, a buckle with motifs of serpent, crane and bamboo, points to the all-important Japanese influence on late nineteenth-century decorative design. The strong colours and composition of the buckle are all directly derived from Japanese prototypes. The Japanese mania which came to be called 'Japonisme' was certainly the single most important contributing factor to Art Nouveau, and a pervasive influence on twentieth-century design.

During the 1860s and '70s, floods of Japanese art and artefacts arrived in Europe when Japan re-opened trade routes with the West after centuries of isolation. Wood cuts, metalwork, ceramics, enamels, amazed and fascinated European artists and designers and led to an entirely new basis for painting and for decorative design. It was the simplicity and economy of line that thrilled Europeans, along with the rich, strong colours and the deep Japanese reverence for nature, depicted with such drama and intensity by the use of simple, strong brushstrokes that captured the essence of the subject without ever actually copying detailed surface ornament.

Japanese art exerted a powerful influence on European artists, particularly on the Impressionists, and on designers in all areas of the applied arts. The Japanese influence turned into a popular mania which became known as aestheticism. Fashionable Victorians added to their

Left: Enamelled jewels enjoyed a new popularity in the 1960s and '70s: the pansy pendant in strong colours with realistic markings; the Pre-Raphaelite wing device, widely used by English Arts and Crafts jewellers, enamelled in the soft lavender-blue so fashionable at the time. Both c.1890-1910. *Above*: An Art Nouveau enamel buckle showing the influence of Japanisme, while the body of the serpent and the bird's neck have been used to convey the meandering Art Nouveau line, c.1890-1900.

21

A turn of the century English pendant of silver and turquoise in the Arts and Crafts manner, incorporating elements of the popular Liberty style and the distinctive stitch motif.

clutter with displays of blue and white porcelain and fans, which became status symbols in interior design. This phenomenon was also an inspiration to Bonté and the horn workers in France, who based their techniques, including the moody and mysterious patina, and their themes of birds, insects and flowers on Japanese traditions. The vital Japanese influence can be seen surfacing throughout the Butler and Wilson repertoire, old and new, particularly in the enormously popular cicada brooches. The cicada motif was taken directly from nineteenth-century Japanese metalwork and unleashed a whole swarm of insect jewels on to the costume jewellery of the 1980s.

The Butler & Wilson collection, with its lively group of insects and creatures, recalls the general popularity of enamelled jewels which re-surfaced in the 1960s and '70s. An intricate pansy pendant in deep purple and white with yellow markings is particularly evocative of the era and its style, and so too is a lavender enamelled pendant in the form of feathered wings, a motif beloved of Arts and Crafts jewellers and of the Pre-Raphaelites.

The silver and amber brooch by Danish silversmith and jeweller Georg Jensen (1866-1935) marks another important contribution to twentieth-century jewellery. An excellent and rare example of its kind, the brooch illustrates the distinctive characteristics that were to bring Jensen fame and success in the 1920s. A cross-breed between Art Nouveau and Art Deco, the sculptural design of this brooch incorporates the highly stylized organic motifs of flowers, leaves and buds interpreted in the usual broad, stumpy but curvaceous manner of this maker. The flowers with their soft petals have long and curling stamens; the pendant buds, attached to the surmount by geometric links, are hung with long amber drops.

Georg Jensen was born near Copenhagen, and served his apprenticeship as a goldsmith, later studying sculpture at the Copenhagen Academy. Around 1895 he made sculptural ceramics, some of which were shown at the 1900 Exposition Universelle in Paris. After 1900, encouraged by the avant-garde painter and metalworker Mogens Ballin, whom he met in the late 1890s, Jensen turned to the design and manufacture of silver and jewellery, and opened a small shop in Copenhagen in 1904. Jensen developed his own personal style, simple, stylized and ornamental, using flowers and fruit as decorative themes. Over the years he collaborated with several talented artists and designers, particularly the painter Johan Rohde, who helped create some of Jensen's most striking and enduring designs.

Silver and amber brooch by Georg Jensen: the highly stylized leaf and flower motifs with curling stamens are in the Art Nouveau mood, amber drops with petal surmounts and malachite beads hang from geometric silver chains, c.1910.

ART DECO

Vogue's stunning editorial photographs encouraged the Art Deco revival of the 1970s by using original accessories like this scarlet enamel powder compact from the 1930s.

Art Deco is the all-embracing term for the decorative style of popular design between the wars. It took its name from the Paris 1925 Exposition Internationale des Arts Décoratifs et Industriels Modernes, which marked the high point of the early Art Deco phase and also the start of a new forward-looking phase called Modernism. Both styles tend to be included under the general label of Art Deco. The most distinctive characteristic of this movement as a whole is a stylish geometry.

The seeds of Art Deco had been planted as early as 1910, as a reaction to the emotive, poetic excesses of Art Nouveau. In Germany and Austria a new branch of the *fin de siècle* art revolution was developing, representing the opposite extreme of the French Art Nouveau style. The basic principles of the unity of the arts and revitalization of the applied or minor arts remained the same, but in creating an entirely new style for a modern world, the Germans and Austrians planned to do away with all unnecessary surface ornament. They worked towards abstract linear forms, sleek architectural lines which were perfectly suited to the function of the object. Again the Japanese influence was evident in structurally disciplined simplicity.

Meanwhile, back in Paris around 1910, disciplined simplicity was certainly not in vogue. The city was still the capital of style, of fashion and untempered luxury. But already, several different factors converged to give birth to the vivacious new style which was later to be called Art Deco. On the one hand, there was a revival of interest in French eighteenth-century design. There was also the powerful influence of avant-garde painters, notably the Fauvists, who painted flat, distorted shapes in hot, strong colours. And in 1910 the magnificent Ballet Russe arrived in Paris, designed by Leon Bakst and directed by Diaghilev, stunning audiences with wild exoticism, passionate scenarios, and sets and costumes created in bold colours, fluid, sensual fabrics and strong vibrant patterns.

The work of the intellectual German designers threw another ingredient into the melting pot in 1910 when the Munich designers held a hugely successful exhibition of their work in Paris. Contemporary influences of travel, speed, communication, the discovery of Tutankhamun's tomb, an obsession with the cinema, a New Rich

Left: Popular fashion jewellery of the 1920s and '30s in powerful abstract designs inspired by the Bauhaus, made of chrome, enamel and bakelite; the stark contrast of red and black complements the strong mechanistic geometric forms.

society, and later African art, Cubism and machines, all contributed elements to the style which emerged as Art Deco.

The pre-1925 style was marked by a strong exoticism, vibrant colour, and mixtures of luxurious materials: in jewellery, coral, jade, onyx, crystal, enamels, and clusters of carved coloured precious stones were mixed together for a look of unprecedented luxury and opulence. Motifs were still largely rococo, classical and representational, incorporating eighteenth-century emblems such as flowers, flower baskets, garlands, drapes and swags; but these gradually became flattened and stylized to conform to the overall rule of geometry. Art Nouveau curves were coaxed into straight lines, into the pure circle or rectangle, and new motifs were chosen either for their geometric qualities, like the sunburst, fountain or lightning ziggurat, or for their relevance to modern life, as in the case of emblems of speed: the arrow, greyhound or gazelle.

After 1925 throughout Europe there was a greater move towards the elimination of all superficial, purely decorative design, and an increasing emphasis on suitability of form to function, on maximum simplicity of line and materials. At this stage Cubism, in its turn inspired by African art, was having a strong effect on decorative design, as was the strict philosophy of the Bauhaus school of design in Germany. From Cubism came the dissection of forms and shapes expressing the position of the object in space, while the functionalism and constructivism of the Bauhaus stressed the simple beauty of the working parts of machines.

The geometry and abstraction of the cubists combined with the metallic angularity of mechanical motifs to produce the rigorous, abstract style that was Modernism. Rich, exotic and colourful materials gave way to chrome, steel and aluminium; colour was suppressed to metallic tones, while smooth planes of polished and engine-turned metal highlighted the angularity of geometric design.

In jewellery these two different stages were also quite distinct, but there was another two-tier system in operation in the 1920s and '30s. On one hand Art Deco was about untempered luxury, appealing to a New Rich layer of society; on the other hand it was about diffusion of design, and a style-conscious New Poor society hit by the severe economic gloom of the 1930s.

Accessories in general, but particularly costume jewellery or less expensive fashion jewellery, thrived in this era. The new breed of working girl, who was fashion-conscious, besotted by the movies, and with some money in her pocket to spend on clothes, created a demand

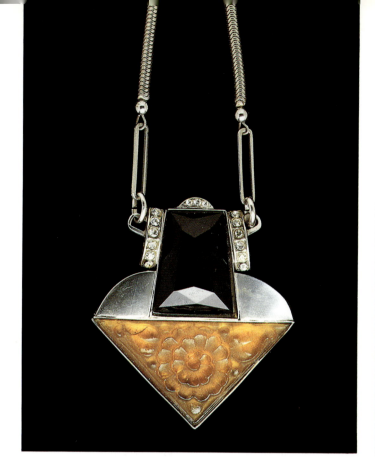

for high fashion jewellery at lower prices. With an eager market the jewellery industry flourished, attracted talented designers and produced inventive and exciting accessories.

Largely due to Lalique's influence, all materials – precious and non-precious – were now at the jeweller's disposal. Factories in France, and especially in the manufacturing centre of Pforzheim in Germany, turned out Art Deco fashion jewellery using semi-precious stones such as chalcedony, cornelian, onyx, chrysoprase, amazonite, and amethyst, mixed with marcasite and set in silver. The dividing line between real and costume jewellery was not as rigid then as it is now; real stones could be set side by side in silver with synthetic stones or glass. Design was all important.

Left: Art Deco pendant using moulded yellow glass in stylized floral forms, mixed with chrome, onyx and paste, c. 1925.
Above: these silver, onyx and ivory earrings in simple geometric forms illustrate the mid-1920s fashion for black and white jewels.

Paul Poiret, the king of Paris couture, had revolutionized women's fashions and changed the entire perception of female form by the start of the Art Deco era. He had freed women from their corsets, loosened the unnatural S-shaped silhouette, reduced the number of underclothes, so that the new fashionable outline was simple, elegant, less structured. He balanced his simple, streamlined shapes with the use of opulent fabrics and textures. Poiret was stunned by the colour and drama of Eastern and Oriental costumes, introduced to Paris by the Ballet Russe. Intoxicated by exoticism, he added turbans, aigrettes and harem pants to his collections in 1910, working in brilliantly coloured and textured silks, brocades and velvets with lashings of gold lamé and rich gold ornamentation. Poiret was also

Butler and Wilson collected Art Deco jewellery made from semi-precious stones in strong colours and abstract designs clearly influenced by Cubism and the Jazz Age, c. 1925-30.

instrumental in bringing fashion and jewels closer together, using jewellery as an essential part of his scheme for drama and opulence.

It was Coco Chanel, the legendary couturier, who was responsible for the change in attitudes towards costume jewellery in the 1920s. Not only did she make fake jewels socially acceptable, even essential for the lady of fashion, but she also showed women how to wear them, turning jewel rules upside down. She encouraged women to change jewellery with their clothes, to wear costume jewels for all occasions, at all times of day, even for the beach. In a parody of the fabulous courtesans bitterly remembered from her youth, Chanel taught women to pile row upon row of *faux* courtly pearls, ball-gown style, incongruously on to casual cardigans and sporty jersey dresses. Fashion designers, alongside the all-important interior designers of the day, set the rules of Art Deco. Fashion and the impression of overall chic triumphed over the staid heirloom syndrome that had governed precious jewellery in the nineteenth century.

It is significant that Butler and Wilson were so attracted to this explosive era. There is certainly a parallel with their own re-education of public taste in the 1980s, when Butler and Wilson made costume jewels socially acceptable, and showed women how to wear them to express their personalities in unexpected, unconventional ways.

Butler and Wilson found that they preferred the chic angularity and strong style of Art Deco to the soft, emotive nineteenth-century qualities of Art Nouveau. Modernism was progressive and forward looking; Art Nouveau was retrospective, steeped in nostalgia. The Art Deco concept of a total design for living, for everything from ashtrays to skyscrapers, from earrings to knives and forks, also appealed to Butler and Wilson, and each piece of inexpensive, Art Deco fashion jewellery they found in the 1960s seemed to be a microcosm of Art Deco or Modernist design.

The Art Deco style was also very much in step with the atmosphere of the early 1970s, overlapping for a while and then following on from the soft, faded hippy craze. In an interview in 1972 with *Women's Wear Daily*, Nicky Butler explained: 'We went into Art Deco because it influences everything that is going on right now. It's much more wearable than anything else and the basic idea is so modern. Art Deco represents the last period of beautifully made objects before the era of mass production. They will always be collectors' items.'

For their own collection Butler and Wilson kept jewellery made from semi-precious materials, in strong colours and designs that are mostly abstract and clearly influenced by Cubism and the Jazz Age. They liked the unexpected juxtaposition of colours and textures: the deep bottle green chrysoprase with rust red cornelian, or chalcedony stained a heavenly heather blue mixed again with cornelian or with shiny black onyx; and shadowy amethyst jostling the strident tones of turquoise.

These stones were always finely cut in bold geometrics and faceted for extra glimmer and shapeliness within the abstract geometric composition. Rock crystal with its icy elegance was often cut into large unusual angular shapes. Two stunning necklaces in the collection are composed of large triangular cut crystals, multi-faceted for added depth and a glacial sparkle, the crisp design completed with crystal and onyx cut into semi-circles, slender rectangles and batons. Another similar necklace is centred with a massive square-cut rock crystal flanked by glittering faceted drum-shaped chrysoprase motifs, crystal half-moons and baton-shaped links.

One of the purest of Art Deco designs in this group is a pendant composed of a rectangular plaque of frosted rock crystal hung from a

Right: Several Art Deco jewels in the collection are made from rock crystal, cut into unexpected geometric shapes, faceted and polished and mixed with richly coloured stones, such as cornelian and blue-stained chalcedony, c.1925-30.

Following pages: The clear contrast of abstract shapes and daring colour combinations of semi-precious stones was a vital ingredient in both modernist and Art Deco design. This collection also shows the popularity of marcasite and the importance of personal and smoking accessories, c.1925-30.

smooth crystal circle and decorated with an emerald-cut amethyst surrounded with steps of steely marcasite and corners of turquoise blue amazonite. Several 'Odeonesque' pendants are designed like frozen waterfalls of black onyx and marcasite; another pendant made of finely faceted slivers of coloured stones and rock crystal gives the impression of the mechanical components of a rolling assembly line. Black was a crucial element in all Art Deco design, black with silver, or with white or red, and in semi-precious jewellery it was rendered by precise slabs of cool black onyx, and occasionally by black moulded glass or by bakelite, to look like carved stone, often mixed with startling red coral; this produced the clear contrasts demanded by abstract art and Art Deco doctrine.

The 1925 Exposition in Paris proved to be an excellent showcase for semi-precious or non-precious jewels of sophisticated, inventive design. Manufacturers showed quantities of stylish enamels, and ingenious mixtures of materials including glass. A firm called Greidenberg exhibited Cubist jewels executed in three-coloured metal, silver plated, gold plated and oxidized, while a designer called Bastard specialized in ivory, horn and mother-of-pearl. The combination of serious, artistic design and fine craftsmanship meant that these jewels were highly desirable and treated with respect.

Marcasite is a natural mineral, iron pyrites, that can be cut and faceted and polished like diamonds. Widely used in the eighteenth century as a substitute for diamonds, it came into its own again during the years between the wars when its steely gleam added a chic and stylish sparkle to semi-precious jewellery. Marcasite jewellery was the speciality of the many manufacturers in Pforzheim, Germany, in the 1930s, the best known being Theodor Fahrner. A manufacturer in the forefront of modern design, he adapted brilliantly from Art Nouveau to Art Deco and then to the cocktail style of the late 1930s and '40s. The Pforzheim industry was flourishing in the years just before World War II, and excellent designs were inspired by Parisian luxury and German modernist ideas.

From the early 1970s Madame Denise Arnal, a long-time jewellery dealer in Paris, regularly searched the flea markets to supply Butler and Wilson with unusual French *bijoux fantaisie* from the 1920s and '30s. She has always respected their very definite avant-garde tastes, and quickly became a close friend and mentor. Madame Arnal understands clearly the different styles that evolved during the inter-war years, as she was growing up in Paris at

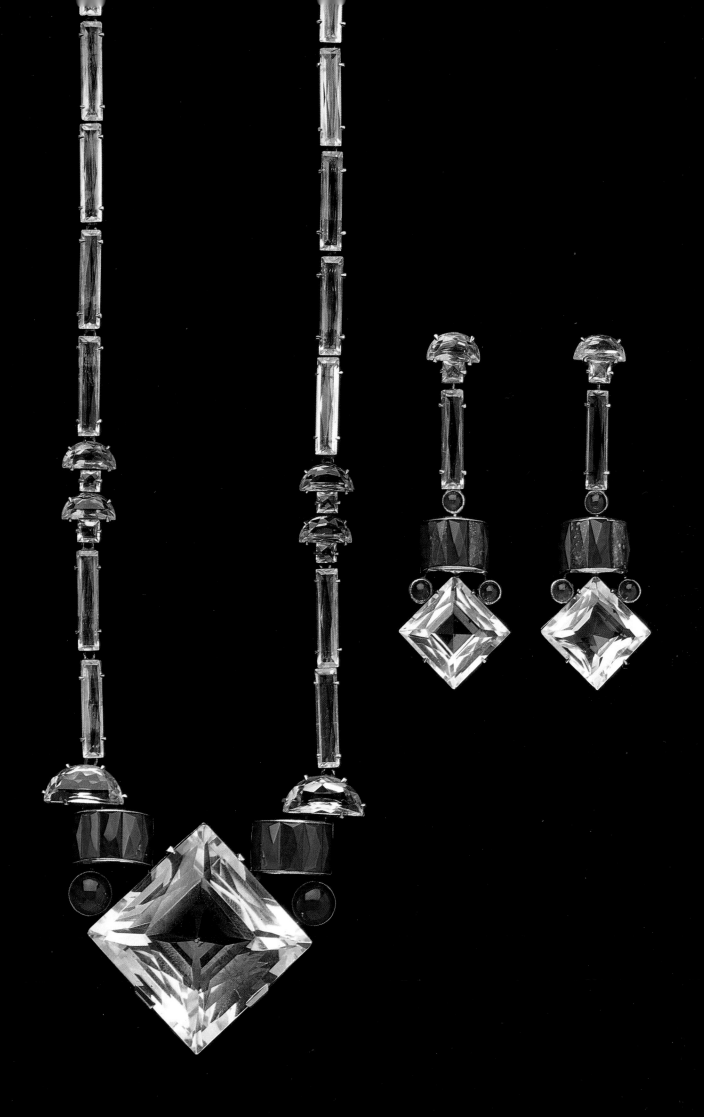

that time. She remembers visiting the 1925 Exhibition in Paris where she was particularly drawn to the jewellery and to the Lalique glass, which she has loved ever since. She was struck at the time by the influence of African art, *l'art nègre*, and by the Colonial Pavilion at the Exhibition.

It was the Jazz Age, and negro jazz bands were all the rage, essential ingredients at any fashionable party. Madame Arnal remembers seeing Josephine Baker, the black nightclub entertainer, the craze of Paris in 1925 and the living embodiment of *l'art nègre*, who danced to packed audiences three times a week in nothing more than a haze of shimmering diamanté. Josephine Baker was to be an important inspiration to Butler and Wilson, and the lively theme of negro jazz bands was one of the first revived by them for their daring new designs in the 1970s.

One of the most inventive areas of Art Deco jewellery – and one that attracted both Madame Arnal in Paris and Butler and Wilson in London – was that of bakelite or early plastic jewellery. The development of plastics in the opening years of the twentieth century was an important factor in the fantasy and originality of fashion jewellery between the wars. Scientific progress in the manufacture of the new and exciting material was timely, since the real jewellery trade was suffering from the economic crises of 1929. As a result of this the costume jewellery industry was flourishing, and crying out for new ideas.

The wistful model in this late 1960s *Vogue* photograph wears modernist chrome and bakelite necklaces of the late 1920s/early '30s.

In the 1930s, plastic was an entirely new and exciting material, with its own properties, qualities and characteristics, and as such it deserved and received respect, being utilized as a material in its own right, and not merely as a substitute for precious substances.

The first commercial plastics had been produced as early as the 1850s in England, but at the time the material was valued most for its ability to imitate horn, tortoiseshell, coral or wood. The development of plastic continued in the 1860s with the discovery of cellulose nitrate, called celluloid, a material with far-reaching application used at the turn of the century for haircombs and other accessories imitating ivory and tortoiseshell. Plastic was a highly prized material and a fashionable novelty at the time. Then in 1907, Leo Baekeland, a Belgian chemist living in the United States, created bakelite, the first totally synthetic plastic, and the one most widely used in Art Deco jewellery. Galalith, the trade name for casein, was also much used; it was a milk-based plastic with versatile decorative possibilities that made it suitable for jewellery and trinkets.

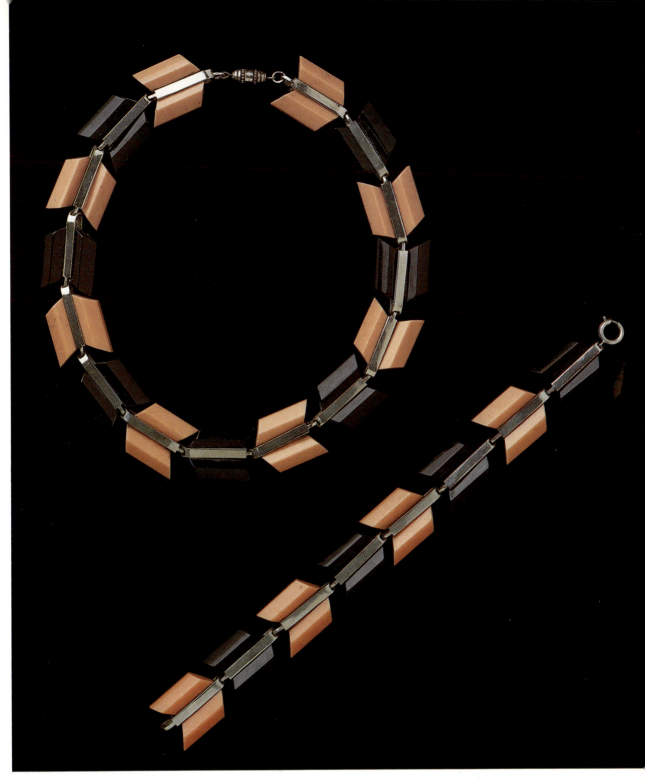

Matching necklace and bracelet of bakelite and chrome in the modernist style, the design based on the popular arrow motif, c.1930.

Plastic jewellery marked the height of freedom of design and manufacture in Art Deco jewellery. Designers limited neither by cost nor by the natural properties of real materials, were able to let their imaginations run riot. The jewels could express the utmost in terms of colour and shape in abstract designs; at the same time, plastic was a witty mimick and could outdo in overall effect the most expensive, extravagant Place Vendôme jewels.

Butler and Wilson appreciated the bakelite and galalith jewellery of the 1930s, enjoying its reflection of the Jazz Age, its adventurous interpretation of sophisticated modern design. They were drawn towards bakelite jewels that were unashamedly plastic, that made the best use of the material, and they collected strong modernist examples, brooches, clips and necklaces that mixed chrome and plastic to achieve a sleek machine-age look. This combination of plastics and chrome epitomized the idea of new materials and the jewellery for the new age.

The cicada that was to become perhaps the best known Butler & Wilson symbol, was very often made during the 1920s and '30s from plastic, with glossy striped and mottled wings and a ridged body. Inspiration for the motif also came from the rich imagination of Elsa Schiaparelli. In Autumn 1938 she had ornamented a sharp suit jacket with large buttons shaped like cicadas, possibly created by Jean Schlumberger. These whimsical creatures functioned as fastenings but also conveyed the timeless ritualistic significance of curious, magical beings from the natural world; in a sense they were Schiaparelli's equivalent of the ancient scarab beetle, sacred symbol of eternity. The cicada, beautifully compact with soft curving wings, gave Butler and Wilson one of their favourite forms for a modern, streamlined depiction of nature.

Constant scouring of markets and antique shops also unearthed splendid bakelite handbags from the Art Deco years, clutch bags in supremely simple and striking modernist designs. Examples in the collection are made with horizontal panels of white boldly contrasting with red, black or blue – their solid, clean, architectural lines anticipating the space-age preoccupation of the 1960s. The French designer Auguste Bonaz created the most exciting modernist jewels of the period, working in bakelite and galalith, within totally streamlined shapes: the pure lines of ovals, squares, circles and oblongs; and implementing the strong colour contrasts of red and black, green and black, blue and white, or black and white.

Bonaz jewels were shown at the 1925 Exhibition, which helped to give both plastics and costume jewellery artistic respectability. These sophisticated jewels in humble materials impressed and influenced Butler and Wilson on their weekly trips to Bermondsey and Portobello Road market. They also pointed the way to the possibility of fine modern design, executed in inexpensive or valueless materials, and to jewellery that cut across the usual barriers of wealth and social status.

Group of 1930s bakelite and metal jewellery in soft, earthy tones that were popular at the time, including some amusing figurative pieces, like the parrot (*below*) and a selection of insects (*right*) which have inspired so many Butler & Wilson originals.

Art Deco

Certain themes from the 1920s and '30s made a particular impact on Butler and Wilson. They liked the high drama and theatrical exoticism of the Egyptian revival craze of the mid-1920s, sparked off by the spectacular discovery of Tutankhamun's tomb by Howard Carter and Lord Caernarvon in 1922. The allure of ancient Egypt swept through the worlds of fashion and design. Sandy or desert coloured dresses were embroidered with hieroglyphics, and evening gowns fell in stiff folds in the Egyptian manner. The craze affected every aspect of life. In 1923 the new model of the Singer sewing machine looked distinctly Pharaonic in design, and it was seriously proposed that the underground extension from Morden to Edgware then under construction should be called Tootancamden, because the line passed through Tooting and Camden Town. Tutankhamun, the young and glamorous king, seemed to embody the modernist spirit.

The most staggering discovery in the tomb was the burial jewellery of the boy-king, and the jewellery world borrowed from it freely for this latest craze. At both ends of the jewellery spectrum – both precious and costume jewellery – the spirit of the ancient Egyptians pervaded design. Van Cleef & Arpels created an exclusive range of diamond jewels set with coloured gems depicting the lives of the Pharaohs, while in Pforzheim the firm of Murrle Bennett followed the same idea for paste jewels, and in New York the Napier company introduced a line of jewels based on the vivid colours and 'bizarre designs' taken from Tutankhamun's treasures, as well as 'cobra' necklaces and 'slave link' bangles.

It was a fashion that lent itself well to exuberant and stagey costume jewellery, which could afford to pander wholeheartedly to such a fleeting whim. Rather than aiming at authenticity, designers heaped their jewels with an indiscriminate medley of motifs: scarabs, hieroglyphs, falcons, Ba-birds, lotus flowers, mummies, Ankh signs, the eye

Egyptian revival silver and enamel brooch in the form of a scarab with outstretched wings in shaded *plique à jour* enamel, probably German, c.1925-30.

of Horus, all depicted in rich colour and detail to obtain an overall effect of intense drama and mystical glamour. Egyptian hieroglyphs, their decorative borders and the heavily stylized figures of wall paintings and papyrus fitted in perfectly with Art Deco geometry.

In costume jewellery, the original inlays were interpreted in bright enamels; the rich gold of the Egyptians was represented most often by silver gilt or gilt metal; and when gemstones were called for they were either genuine semi-precious stones such as lapis lazuli, cornelian and turquoise, or glass coloured to produce the same effect. Brooches, often in the shape of the winged scarab, were extremely popular, while larger pendants and dramatically complicated necklaces fringed with enamelled symbols and charms recalled the ancient immense funerary pectorals.

Shaded *plique à jour* enamel, in which the German manufacturers particularly excelled, was very often used on high-fashion Egyptian revival jewellery. It is interesting that such a complex and difficult technique, requiring a high degree of skill, was used on inexpensive whimsical ornaments. *Plique à jour* was particularly effective when used for the spread wings of the Ba-bird, the falcon or the scarab.

For their collection Butler and Wilson have kept jewels that best combined the rich Egyptian influence with the lean Art Deco style, choosing pieces that incorporate *plique à jour* enamels. One large brooch is shaped as a winged scarab, and its curving spread wings in shaded *plique à jour* recall the monumental breast ornaments of the ancient Egyptians. Large winged scarabs were traditionally placed over the hearts of the dead, inscribed with a text from the Book of the Dead to ensure that the heart did not give evidence against its owner during the last judgment. A wide bracelet, in typical 1920s form, is also based on the scarab motif, composed of a series of superbly formalized beetles, their bodies formed of hardstones, their wings and surrounds made of *plique à jour* studded with marcasite.

The scarab motif again forms the central theme for this Egyptian revival bracelet in silver and enamel, c. 1925-30.

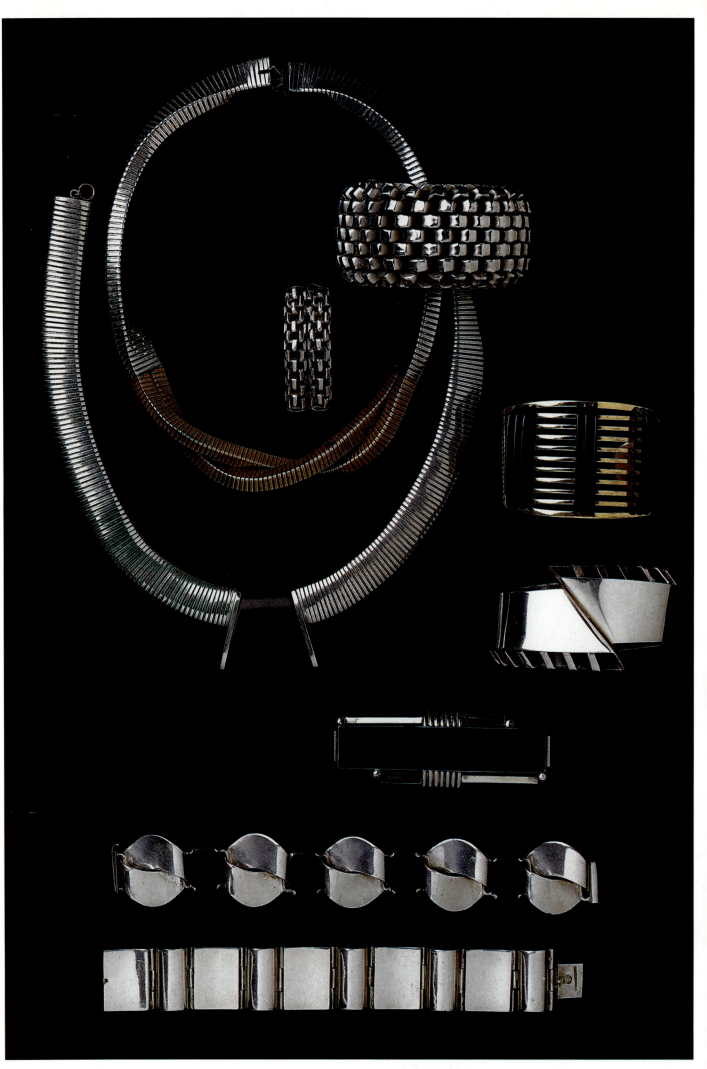

THE COCKTAIL JEWELS

The cocktail style of jewellery that emerged around 1937 at the end of the Art Deco period also influenced Butler and Wilson, though to a lesser extent than the style of 1925. The Butler & Wilson collection continues to illustrate the development of twentieth-century jewellery design with some choice examples of the cocktail style, showing how the fashion evolved naturally from the austere geometric modernist ornaments of the previous decade.

As a reaction to the stark abstraction of design, the flat two-dimensional compositions, the suppression of colour and the use of cool metallic tones, jewellery in the late 1930s began slowly to blossom again. Severe architectural lines were softened into more voluptuous curves, plumped up into sculptural three dimensional forms, and slowly coaxed into figurative elements.

Movement crept back into design, but now it was a frozen movement, stiff but fluid at the same time, encompassing the fascinating blend of opposing elements that characterizes 1940s design: a new feminine softness in the form of ribbons, bows, drapes and flowers was combined with the unrelenting toughness of mechanical motifs. Early cocktail jewels of the late 1930s tended still to look geometric, rather like bulkier versions of Art Deco pieces, but gradually they became softer, more full of movement and texture as the 1940s progressed and the style developed its own personality.

As always in jewellery history, the style was inextricably linked to the atmosphere of its age and to the position of women in society, their fashions and their own attitudes towards their femininity. Cocktail jewellery was jewellery to show off in. It was extravagant, bubbly, bold and bossy and its voluptuousness and colour surely reflected women's independence and confidence along with the new curvaceous femininity that replaced the androgyny of Art Deco.

Left: Group of machine-age jewels, of chrome and bakelite, showing the gradual transition from Art Deco and modernism to the more forceful mechanistic style of the late 1930s and '40s.

A Butler & Wilson revival of one of the most typical motifs of the cocktail style: the voluptuous ribbon bow.

The Cocktail Jewels

The theme of machinery in motion spilled over from the 1930s into the next decade to become the most dominant influence on jewellery design. Bracelets, brooches and necklaces incorporated motifs reminiscent of ball bearings, girders, pipes and rods, the moving staircase or escalator, the rolling rhythm of the assembly line or the tank. Movement, in both design and manufacture, was the most important characteristic of the jewellery of this period. Gold jewels were ingeniously engineered with fine clasps and hinges, and constructed like flexible brickwork, a strong feature of the examples in the Butler & Wilson collection. A gold necklace and two bracelets of finely engineered articulated links move with a slinky flexibility; they look like machine-age jewels but have the feel of silky ribbons.

In contrast to the slender platinum settings for diamonds in the 1920s, there was a move towards the use of wider expanses of metal in designs, sculpted into softer more curvaceous shapes; sweeps of rose pink gold and bright buttery yellow gold. Colour became all-important once again, but it was very different from the hard, bright theatrical exoticism of Art Deco. Now jewellers concentrated on subtlety, using coloured gold and semi-precious stones.

The large ribbon bracelet in flexible goldwork, a speciality of Van Cleef & Arpels, is an example of one of the most popular construction techniques of the period, a perforated pattern of either little hexagons, which created a honeycomb effect, or little overlapping semi-circles, which gave the impression of slinky scales. Very often in Van Cleef & Arpels jewels, each little shape was fixed with a tiny diamond, ruby or sapphire in a star-shaped setting. This bracelet focuses on the woven goldwork, and has a flounced buckle fastening. The buckle motif with its polished curved flap folding over a rod or tube was another favourite feature of 1940s bracelets. The second bracelet is also an outstanding

Rose gold was an important feature of 1940s jewellery, along with superbly engineered and articulated flexible goldwork, as shown by these three gold bracelets, c.1940.

Right: Group of precious jewels illustrating the most evocative elements of 1940s cocktail jewellery: the flexible brickwork on the tie necklace, the use of little rows of rubies, the buckle motif, massive gold bracelets designed to capture the effect of a moving staircase or an assembly line, c.1940.

The Cocktail Jewels

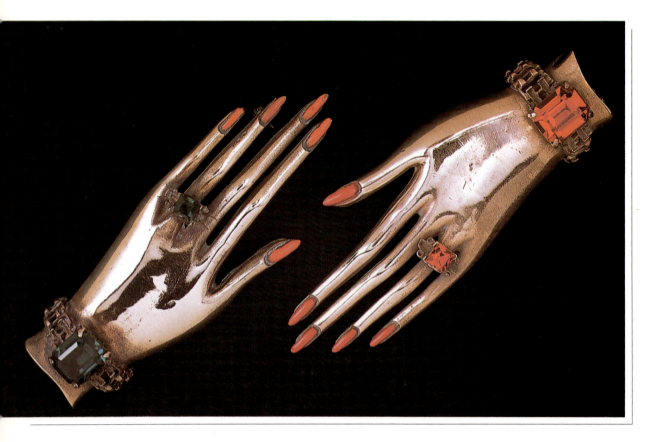

example of a typical form, strong links of mechanical design fitted together with fine articulation to resemble an assembly line or tank track.

The brickwork necklace, in the form of a tie, incorporates a highly formalized ribbon-bow motif ornamented with geometrically cut rubies. Cocktail jewellery went on to explore exuberant stylized floral motifs, quirky figures such as ballerinas, scarecrows and gardeners, and used masses of huge translucent semi-precious stones, but Butler and Wilson's taste veered towards a more architectural style.

The disembodied hand, either bejewelled in costume jewellery versions, or holding a rose, as in precious jewels, was a favourite theme in the late 1930s and '40s. Clearly inspired by surrealism, this curious vision also derived from Victorian jewellery design in which the hand, elaborately cuffed, holding a flower, a wreath, a fruit basket or a love letter, was a favourite motif: the hand of friendship.

In Paris in the 1930s in the midst of an obsession with novelty and newness, there was also a craze for Victoriana, especially its more 'kitsch' aspects, and hand jewels in gilt metal, ivory or jet, were among the trinkets and curiosities hunted down in the flea markets. In the late 1930s at the start of the cocktail era, Cartier produced a series of hand jewels, the hand carved from black onyx holding a coral flower, while in the world of costume jewellery the fashion was represented by elaborate gilt versions, like the example in the Butler & Wilson collection.

Early in their repertoire, Butler and Wilson revived this favourite gilt hand brooch from the 1940s, with its slender, tapering fingers and painted fingernails, gem-set ring and bracelet, and later in the 1980s, their oversized, surreal diamante version proved a popular success.

Although there are no examples in the Butler & Wilson collection, the opulent fantasy jewels made from the late 1940s to the '60s, and epitomized by the work of Duc Fulco di Verdura and Jean Schlumberger, provided rich inspiration for the Butler & Wilson originals of the 1980s. Both Verdura and Schlumberger had started their careers by creating fashion jewellery in Paris in the 1920s and '30s, Verdura for Chanel, Schlumberger for Schiaparelli, a training that allowed them to explore the full potential of fantasy jewellery. Both left Paris to work as 'real' jewellers in New York, and unhampered by traditional training and preconceptions, they both – in entirely separate and individual ways – set about designing fantasy jewels in precious materials, mixing colours, textures and gemstones, and revitalizing archetypal motifs to achieve the modern but dreamlike ornaments of a vibrant fantasy world. In a sense, Butler and Wilson have led costume jewellery back on to this path towards the joyful dreamworld that jewellery should inhabit.

The desembodied hand was a favourite decorative theme in the late 1930s and '40s and one that has been revived and re-interpreted by Butler and Wilson, either in the style of 1940s originals (*left*) or in updated late 1980s guise oversized and covered in diamanté.

BUTLER & WILSON
REVIVALS

Around 1970 Butler and Wilson's tantalizing stand in Antiquarius, 'not much bigger than a closet', as one journalist wrote at the time, was crammed from floor to ceiling with enticing, decorative jewels illustrating a gamut of twentieth-century vogues. Butler and Wilson's tastes were somewhat offbeat from the mainstream, but extremely well defined. They have always been very certain about the jewellery they like and dislike. The decorative jewels hanging on the walls and crowded in the showcases in a seductive clutter had been passionately plucked from the choicest dealers' stocks in London and Paris. Connoisseurs recognized the quality and scope of the selection.

There were long Victorian and Edwardian muff chains, in gilt metal or set with stones or crystals, rich crosses, endless rows of beads — ivory, amber and coloured hardstones, always ungraduated — armfuls of ivory bangles and bakelite bracelets. There were Victorian and Edwardian beaded bags in the rich colours of faded grandeur, and 1920s evening purses of shimmering metallic mesh, plastic *minaudières* (or fitted evening bags) with silk tassels. Art Deco cigarette cases in enamels or eggshell lacquer sat beside gilt metal and enamel Art Deco brooches, buckles and clips; and a wall was pinned with gleaming butterflies, mostly in deep glossy enamels, some in carved horn or moulded plastics of the 1920s, others made of silver with wings of bright silvery blue butterfly-wing preserved under crystal: a peculiarly Victorian phenomenon. Hovering with these were other insects, birds and animals in all materials.

Art Deco and Modernist plastics in violent colours mingled with Art Nouveau horn pendants and enamelled buckles, brooches and pendants, and with the pieces of Victorian Whitby jet, and the shinier, sharper and more delicate French jet, which was really black glass, cut and faceted to create glittering petal-laden pendants, brooches and earrings.

As demand for all these period treasures quickly exceeded supply, Butler and Wilson began to produce silver and enamel reproductions or modern versions of their favourite Art Deco cubist figural forms: little angular swinging golfers, tennis players, chic windswept ladies pulling greyhounds behind them, the head and shoulders of a sailor (taken from the decoration on a 1920s cigarette case), black jazz musicians and pairs of dancers, a jaunty 'Biggles' character with cap and goggles.

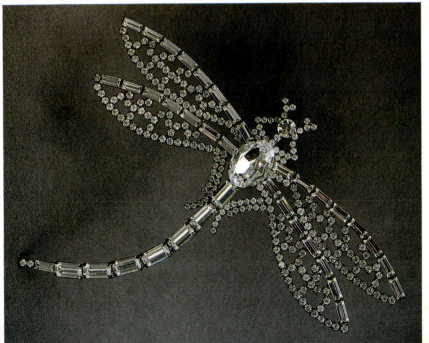

Above: Silver and enamelled insects in the Art Nouveau style were amongst Butler and Wilson's first revivals in the early 1970s.
Left: A late 1980s reworking of a favourite turn of the century theme: the curvaceous dragonfly in dazzling diamanté.

The distinctive image of the '20s tennis player was based on Suzanne Lenglen, who at the age of fifteen became the tennis champion of France, famed for her sensational leaps and athleticism, for her particular style of free and easy dressing, the long cardigans over a pleated skirt, the wide band around her head. She became a huge star, and a celebrity in England as well as in France; she represented modern life and the new sporting women. She also served as the model for Cocteau's tennis player in his ballet of 1924, *Le Train Bleu*, for which Chanel designed the costumes.

In the ballet the passengers on the 'Train Bleu' form a synthesis of modern life. They included gigolos, prostitutes and the beautiful young things of the new age. Since sport was such an important part of this new life, along with the tennis player, who was danced by Nijinska, there was also a golfer, supposedly modelled on the figure of the Prince of Wales, the future Edward VIII and Duke of Windsor. The stylish images of these figures from the ballet inspired popular jewels around 1925, and it is a tribute to the universality of the characters that their recreations were just as popular some fifty years later.

Butler and Wilson's versions, all taken from originals, were cast and enamelled and at first all the work was carried out by their repairers. The little brooches were made in very small quantities as an experiment. They proved a great success; Butler & Wilson revivals were launched.

They went on to make more ambitious buckles, brooches and pendants in the Art Nouveau style, choosing the classic symbols of Art Nouveau iconography, world-weary flowers, serpents, swans and dragonflies wrapped in the sinuous curving lines synonymous with the movement. These were all enamelled in deep, rich colours. Around the same time, they started reworking old elements into new pieces, fixing old buckles to new belts and incorporating old beads into new chokers.

New pieces of jewellery were added only very gradually to the existing stock of period jewellery. In the meantime Butler and Wilson were constantly on the lookout for aspects of antique and twentieth-

Left: Butler and Wilson's collection of late Victorian and Edwardian French jet, the shiny black glass immaculately cut, faceted and polished, c.1890-1910.

In the 1980s Butler and Wilson updated the fashion for jet, mixing old and new, piling on the pzazz with row upon row of scintillating black glass beads.

Two early Art Deco revivals based on the theme of the female face: (*top*) a stylish face in painted ceramics; (*below*) a vision of speed and modern femininity in metal and diamanté, stars embedded in her streaming hair.

century jewellery which they could present in a fresh fashion-orientated way. In the early 1970s the mania for bug brooches began and again Butler and Wilson bought old examples whenever they could and supplemented the supply with some modern versions. It was the slim cicada with folded translucent wings, popular in bakelite jewellery in the 1930s, that most appealed to Butler and Wilson. To reaffirm this image, which has remained a perennial favourite in all their shops, the motif was depicted in plastics, metal, later in diamanté, and even in ceramic when they discovered huge ceramic cicada wall ornaments and planters at a factory in Vallauris in the South of France.

In 1973 they focused on the soft lustrous and silky gleam of mother-of-pearl jewellery. Following in a long line of unusual materials ranging from coral and ivory to volcanic lava, mother-of-pearl was popular for inexpensive fashion jewellery, love tokens and

novelties in the late nineteenth century. This pearlescent shell had been the main component of exquisite trinkets known as Palais Royale wares in seventeenth-century Paris, and these treasured accessories were still being made 200 years later. The taste for mother-of-pearl was revived at the turn of the century with the interest in humble but beautiful materials encouraged by Arts and Crafts and other artistic revolutions. Nineteenth-century mother of pearl could be very finely carved or more crudely cut depending on the age and quality of the jewel. Favourite designs included little fans, intricately carved and pierced, the cuffed hand of friendship which was one of the most popular of Victorian sentimental motifs, flowers, leaves, fruit and berries.

In the 1970s mother-of-pearl was given a new lease of life and the glistening little brooches were promoted from downstairs to upstairs jewels as they became favourite accessories of fashion-conscious clients. Butler and Wilson

These silver and enamelled brooches were best sellers in the 1970s, inspired by cubist sporty figures of the 1920s, the sailor, golfer, tennis player; (*below*) this motorist with goggles provides a strong image of speed and the frivolous fast living of the years between the wars.

To recreate the atmosphere of the Jazz Age, Butler and Wilson produced silver and enamelled brooches in the form of negro jazz bands and stylish dancers.

gathered together an extensive group of luminous mother-of-pearl jewels and objects and presented them in an exciting way, encouraging fashion editors, particularly Caroline Baker at *Nova*, to photograph the group in a sensual, tempting setting which showed them in an entirely new and modern light.

The tactile, shiny materials and glorious colours of beads had always captivated Butler and Wilson and through the 1970s, they continued to buy and sell old and new beads. Alongside Edwardian and 1920s golden amber and creamy ivory beads, almost always ungraduated, they displayed new beads, of agates, rose quartz and cornelian. Many of these cut and polished coloured stones were supplied by the old Cornish Stone Company, established in Cornwall in the early years of this century. During buying trips in London, Brighton and around the country, Butler and Wilson had often come across the name of the Cornish Stone Company, and now they set out to trace its various branches all over Great Britain. They bought up old stocks and made them into strings of beads with all the charm of the old and the fashion element of the new.

Butler and Wilson have always shown women how to wear costume jewellery, and here the classic cicada brooch is presented 1980s style; *below* a gilt and enamel revival of the motif with stylized soaring wings; (*bottom*) this *Vogue* photograph of the early 1970s matches amber with an Art Deco bakelite bangle.

As Butler and Wilson gained confidence and momentum with their jewellery manufacturing they began to add more original ideas to their repertoire of reworked and revived jewellery. Around the mid 1970s they decided to revive one of their favourite romantic motifs, Pierrot, the French pantomime character beloved of the 1920s. Pierrot was the French adaptation of, or improvisation on, Arleccino, the Harlequin character from the Italian Commedia dell'Arte. Throughout the nineteenth century he had been a favourite subject for romantic painters following in the tradition of Watteau, whose dreamy, theatrical subjects often included reflective, melancholy portrayals of Pierrot.

In the 1920s and '30s the romantic Pierrot captured public imagination and reflected the spirit of the age, a charming link with the past in the midst of the upsurge of modernity. Pierrot and his female counterpart and partner Pierrette are immediately recognizable by their pure white costumes symbolizing purity and light. Pierrot is the sad clown, a lovelorn and lyrical figure, white-faced with melancholy, in a baggy white costume, traditionally with three huge black buttons, a frill or ruff around the neck, and on his head a tight-fitting black cap. One solitary glistening tear hangs on his pale cheek, the symbol of sadness, of lost love, as he plays a mandolin and sings beneath a pale moon.

Cosmopolitan picked up Butler and Wilson's Pierrot revival of the 1970s.

The black and white costumes of Pierrot and Pierrette conformed to the vogue for black and white in fashion and decoration in the mid-1920s. This endearing clown was a recurring image in the decorative arts of the decade, and popularity for him grew to be something of a mania, a passion that was revived in the 1970s as different aspects of Art Deco were gradually revealed. Occasionally Pierrots were used for brooches and jewels, but more often they were immortalized as porcelain figurines and small objects.

A romantic and whimsical Pierrot brooch.

Butler and Wilson made a series of porcelain objects, figures, mirrors, ashtrays, dishes, porcelain brooches and plastic jewels bearing the Pierrot legend. Using as models the objects they found at big antiques fairs outside Paris, Butler and Wilson worked with potteries in Stoke-on-Trent to recreate Pierrot ceramics. This is one example of their persistence in finding the right people and factories to make jewels and objects. They have always maintained that any techniques that have been used before can still be carried out just as well today.

In the Pierrot range, there were also small silver brooches of stylized Pierrot faces, perhaps with sparkling diamanté caps, the design taken from

a period piece. Bangles were made in pale plastics with the figure of Pierrot stretching around the bangle while ivory pink plastic necklaces showed Pierrot playing the mandolin, clutching a single red rose, sitting alone and wistful on a swing, under the full moon, or perched in a crescent moon.

Original Pierrot objects, like these highly stylized cigarette cases (*left/right*) and the silver and enamel belt buckle, (*above left*) inspired the range of Pierrot revivals.

Butler and Wilson adapted the charming mask motif derived from the Pierrot legend to make modern brooches in enamels and diamanté.

As part of the same romantic mood Butler and Wilson began to make jewels representing the jovial creased face of the man in the moon, and crescent moons and stars, a favourite and enduring theme that has been used in several different styles and guises throughout their twenty-one years. The man in the moon appeared in late Victorian and Edwardian jewels, most characteristically and effectively carved from moody blue-tinged moonstone often cupped in a diamond-set crescent, creating one of the most charming and sought after emblems in jewellery iconography.

In 1979, when Butler & Wilson's design won the competition for that year's Christmas lights in Regent Street, it was these golden crescent moons and shooting stars of moonlit romance that the jewel designers had chosen for their theme. As with their jewels, it was a timeless classic subtly updated to catch the mood of the day. The design and production of the lights was an important exercise for Butler and Wilson, as they had to change, overnight, from working in miniature to an oversized scale. Their ideas and designs converted so successfully

A group of playful Pierrots, combined with the Man in the Moon motif, recreated in pale pink plastic, set with diamanté, at the height of the romantic craze in the mid-1970s.

to the new medium that the lights were used again the following year, an unprecedented choice.

These relics of romance were signs that the 1970s had brought a return to all things natural. In fashion this trend was marked by dreamy floral prints and mixed patterns, by soft floating layered clothes and

The Christmas light display at the Harrods 21st anniversary exhibition in 1989; and (*right*) the Regent Street Christmas lights, created by Butler and Wilson in 1979.

long loose and rippling Pre-Raphaelite style hair. The back-to-nature, back-to-handicraft ethic corresponded to the Arts and Crafts movement of exactly one hundred years earlier. Around 1976–7, in order to suit this romantic, natural climate Butler and Wilson came up with their most ambitious idea thus far: glass flower jewels.

On their visits to antique markets they had come across old pieces of French or Venetian glass in the form of leaves, fruits and flowers, probably originally used for chandeliers. Butler and Wilson managed to buy an old factory stock of glass flowers and fruits and reworked these deeply coloured near-opaque glass elements into complex naturalistic necklaces, full of movement and energy, tinged with the poetic flavour of Art Nouveau, yet reminiscent of the colourful chaos of English country gardens. The glass leaves were in strong grass green, the flowers in vibrant red and purple, or yellow with orange tipped stamens. Some leaves and stems were made from threaded tiny green glass beads.

The necklaces were totally different from any jewellery available at that time. Non-precious, highly decorative and colourful, these new necklaces drew attention to the wearer's individuality; they became focal points, and so much more than appendages to clothes, drawing the fashion limelight away from clothes on to the jewels themselves. In

Shooting stars, crescent moons and planets have remained popular themes in many Butler & Wilson collections through the 1970s and '80s.

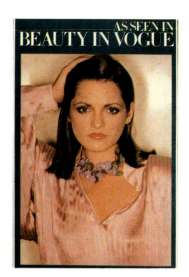

Above: A necklace worn for a *Vogue* beauty shot.
Right: The ambitious glass flower necklaces, reminiscent of chaotic English country gardens, were entirely new creations. Made from old Venetian glass elements, these suited the romantic mood of the 1970s (*above*). A group of equally ambitious blown glass jewels in deep, rich gem-like colours (*below*).

1978 the Observer magazine asked Sir Cecil Beaton to photograph actress Lesley-Anne Down wearing romantic clothes by English designers, accessorized by a deep red cherry glass necklace and earrings from Butler & Wilson. The flower jewels could not have been in sharper contrast to the prevailing conventional taste for discreet gold chains, gold studs, and the plainest, least-ornamental jewellery ever known in the history of jewels.

In 1980 there were early signs of a boom in the market for sophisticated accessories, and Butler and Wilson came up with an unexpected fashion for ethnic-style jewellery, sexy and savage. They turned back to their original love of beads, this time revamping the image, using the hot tones of coral and amber, as well as new glass beads specially made in rich, earthy colours, strung with shells and gilt leaves for a raunchy desert island look.

Endlessly experimenting with new ideas and techniques, in 1985 Butler and Wilson devised a range of colourful jewellery that was both unusual and intricate. This time, the glass was not beaten in an ordinary way, but instead it was blown into the metal framework of the jewel to achieve a very delicate effect. In fact, the finished jewel looked like carefully-set gems rather than glass. The processes involved were extremely complicated, requiring not only time and skill but also the setting up of a special glass-making section in the factory. The jewels were exquisite, many of them in floral forms, a single open blossom or a luscious spray, huge brooches and earrings in church window colours that caught the light spectacularly.

Butler and Wilson had long been attracted to Victorian Scottish jewellery and in 1982 they felt that the time was right for another Celtic revival, this time using old jewels to create an entirely modern fashion. Victorian Scottish jewels represented some of the most traditional centuries-old Celtic designs but by the time Butler and Wilson had amassed a dazzling collection and presented them, not with the usual tweeds, but with silks or a tuxedo, they seemed to be the newest accessory in town.

The prosperous mid-Victorians with their insatiable appetite for novelties, trinkets and jewels, turned traditional Scottish 'folk' jewellery into a major high-fashion accessory of the 1860s. The intense early Victorian atmosphere of Romanticism bred a preoccupation with the past, with history – a somewhat glamorized history – and with stories of the Middle Ages, of kings and queens, and knights and chivalry and the nobility of love. Famous historical novels of the time,

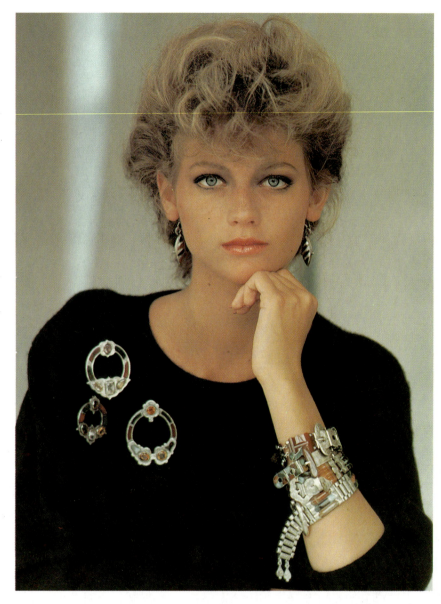

The new look for old jewels, modelled by actress Sophie Ward, and (*right*) examples from Butler & Wilson's personal collection of Victorian Scottish jewellery, with their mossy coloured agates superbly cut and set in traditional Celtic styles, c. 1860-1880.

particularly those by Sir Walter Scott, stirred the public imagination and influenced fashions and jewels.

The young Queen Victoria epitomized the romanticism of the 1830s and '40s; although she was never a fashion leader, she exerted an enormously strong influence on public tastes. She was especially fond of Scotland and when she acquired Balmoral Castle in 1848 the highest seal of approval was set on all things Scottish. Scotland with its lochs and mountains, its massive castles, heather and swirling mists, the heraldry that ruled the clans, offered untold romantic possibilities. It became a fascination almost to the point of obsession with the Victorians. It was a favoured spot for tourists, especially for honeymooners; it offered opportunities for country walks and nature rambles and the study of specimens that became a popular hobby at this time;

the Queen's children wore tartans, and her guests at a ball to mark the opening of the 1851 Exhibition were all required to wear Scottish costume. In the 1860s, the craze for tartan and Scottish jewels – first glimpsed in England in 1822 when George IV donned full highland dress – swept both England and France, where *robes écossaises* were all the rage worn with bracelets enamelled in imitation of tartan ribbon.

A flourishing tourist industry conspired with the growing English fashion for Scottish jewellery to keep Edinburgh jewellers busy, industriously creating new ideas and models. They were followed hotfoot by the enterprising Birmingham industry where most Victorian Scottish jewellery was produced. They made jewels of Scottish 'pebbles' or agates, of mellow earthy tones, set in elaborately chased silver settings based on traditional, often ancient designs. Some early jewels were authentic facsimiles of medieval jewels or items of regalia, but as with all Victorian vogues, styles were gradually adapted to Victorian themes and tastes, and diluted or augmented to attract a wider clientele.

Between the 1860s and the turn of the century, huge quantities of Scottish jewels were turned out in Edinburgh and Birmingham, and although so much was produced, the quality is superb. Designs are varied, intricately detailed, finely proportioned and often ingenious. The soft heathery colours of the stones are deep and moody and mix perfectly with the heavy and noble settings.

The most popular traditional shapes included the circular ring brooch based on ancient and medieval examples, as well as brooches shaped like plaid or kilt pins in the form of daggers or dirks, shields and basket-hilted swords. These designs might also be embellished with a thistle, baronial crests, the cross of St Andrew, or the strap and buckle which often surrounded the emblem of the clan's chieftain, and also referred to Queen Victoria's position as Head of the Order of the Garter. Ring or annular brooches had been worn in Scotland from the second century BC, and after dazzling archaeological finds of early Celtic jewels, ring brooches and other ancient forms became a major inspiration for nineteenth-century designs. Hearts were popular in Scottish folk jewels from the early eighteenth century, when crowned 'Luckenbooth' brooches, sold in locked booths around St Giles's Kirk, Edinburgh, were given as love tokens and also as protection against evil spirits. The design, which emphasized the romantic undercurrent of the whole fashion, was much imitated in the 1800s.

As the fashion gathered momentum, the basic ingredients were adapted to 'South-of-the-Border' Victorian fashions that had less to do

Flexible Victorian Scottish bracelets, of beautifully shaped links of agates in all colours, set in chased silver borders, several of them with the popular strap and buckle motif taken from the Order of the Garter, c. 1860-1890.

with national regalia. Flexible bracelets were made of beautifully shaped links of agates in all colours, set in chased silver borders, or occasionally in gold, and fastened with a padlock or often with a buckle. On some examples the buckle was just decoration, on others the bracelet slipped through the buckle to fasten just like a belt.

The increasingly sophisticated designs of the 1890s had even more tenuous links with Scotland. The pieces tended to be much simpler, stylized, with clean-cut outlines and a marked absence of elaborate chased silver mounts. The agates of these brooches were set very precisely to present one perfectly even surface representing shapes such as a single leaf, a ribbon bow, shell or butterfly. Novelty brooches incorporated typical Victorian motifs, such as the anchor, the sentimental pansy symbolizing 'thoughts', or the little Scottish rowing boat with crossed oars.

The coloured agates quarried in different parts of Scotland give this jewellery its distinctive character. The 'pebbles' used included bloodstone, cornelian, jasper, granite, malachite, moss agate, and countless other agates in warm mossy tones and patterned in natural striations. A particular variation of Scottish pebble jewellery was made of pale pink Corennie and grey Aberdeen granites, usually in simple geometric patterns. Heavily striated grey agate was particularly popular in all of this jewellery, and was often mixed with amber coloured citrines, also known as Cairngorms. Citrines were also often paired with pale amethysts, and both might be cut and carved into thistle shapes. Rock crystals were much used, sometimes as very large central stones in a circular plaid brooch.

The deep colours of the stones required imposing settings. The mounts were elaborately chased in foliate or scroll designs, recalling medieval metalwork or sometimes decorated with Celtic interlacing or pierced in a Gothic openwork design. The little curling leaves of thistles were heavily textured and three dimensional in high relief.

One of the attractions of Victorian Scottish jewellery is the consistently high standard of production, which demonstrates superb workmanship, fine attention to detail and precision in stone cutting and setting. The stones were sliced thinly, cut into the required shape and then set into a mount already prepared. The stones were usually sent to Idar Oberstein in Germany to be cut and polished.

For their own collection Butler and Wilson have kept back the richest examples of brooches and bracelets, choosing the most beautiful stones, immaculately set with stunning colour combinations, including several strap-and-buckle or garter bracelets, with buckles in curved

When Butler and Wilson presented antique Scottish jewels worn casually and unexpectedly with silks or a tuxedo they became the newest accessories in town. *Far right:* A traditional dirk-shaped brooch showing the immaculate cutting and setting of stones and the use of beautiful moss agate in this highly detailed brooch, c.1860.

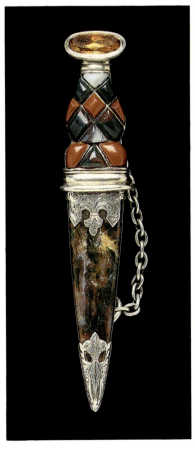

Gothic shapes, elaborately chased, and others with large central motifs, shaped and pierced and set with citrines. The strap-and-buckle motif also features prominently on brooch designs, while others incorporate a star motif, its modern simplicity a perfect foil to the intricate chasing of the silver. Charming, evocative brooches shaped as dirks and swords and a sword crossed with a shield, a heraldic symbol, inspired Butler and Wilson's own 1980s Celtic revival.

Moving across continents and cultures, from one strong tradition to another, Butler and Wilson also introduced the wild Navajo look to the fashions of 1982. From the mid-1970s Nicky Butler had been travelling widely in the United States, particularly in California and in New Mexico, and had been captivated by the powerful, ritualistic styles of the native Pueblo Indians. The strong image of the Red Indian, fuelled by the movies, had always fascinated Butler and Wilson, and the theme has remained an inspiration from the time of their earliest productions up to the present day. The Red Indian head with an extravagant feathered headdress was depicted in the 1970s in carved ivory, and in the late 1980s in dazzling diamanté and coloured pastes.

Self-decoration has always been an important element in the American Indian culture and their distinctive style of silver and turquoise jewellery also had deep spiritual and ritualistic significance. There was an immensely long and rich tradition of metalwork in the early American civilizations and those of South and Central Mexico. The turquoise, found in the southern part of North America, was used

A quick change in cultures and civilizations: ethnic, exotic beads in deep, earthy colours are worn as long earrings seen on the cover of *Harpers & Queen* (*above*) while the Red Indian design inspires a riotously coloured gemset headdress of the late 1980s (*right*).

Far right: A highly stylized Mexican silver, turquoise and hardstone brooch in the Butler & Wilson collection, c. late 1930s or '40s, inspiration for the wild Navajo look of the 1980s.

BUTLER & WILSON REVIVALS

Exotic sharkskin bangles in soft, muted shades taken up by *Vogue* in 1983.

originally by the Aztecs and then later by the Pueblo Indians, who actually worked the deposits to find this magical material, the colour of the sky, which they then made into spectacular jewellery.

Butler and Wilson bought old and new Navajo jewellery, hand wrought in silver and set with massive slabs of sky blue turquoise, often streaked with jagged black matrix, in smooth or craggy shapes. There were wide bangles, with heavy or openwork silver, many with twisted rope decoration, or silver with Aztec patterns, and belts of leather, silver and turquoise.

While they were in the mood for spectacular colour and materials, Butler and Wilson stocked the shop with huge, glossy amber beads and coral, both of which they had originally discovered in antique markets and had always appreciated and enjoyed. This was also the time for promoting exotic sharkskin bangles, in soft, muted pastel shades, or deeper tones, a fashion taken up by *Vogue* in 1983. This tactile, sensual material in tints of green and pink was widely used for luxury objects, boxes, cigarette cases, powder compacts in the 1930s, and was now revitalized and recycled for jewellery of the 1980s.

Previous pages: Group of silver, turquoise and obsidian jewels in the naive, ritualistic style of Mexican or American Indian jewellery popular in the early 1980s.

Both Mexico and the wild west have been important influences on Butler & Wilson design, providing amusing ideas for many different collections.

Right: The new primitive jewels of the early 1980s were an integral part of this sexy desert island look shown by *Harpers & Queen*.

These years of invention and experimentation and gradual re-education of taste had paved the way for the massive explosion of costume jewellery that took place around 1982. Fashion editors of magazines and newspapers could write of nothing else; costume jewellery and glittering fakes looked set to become the fashion phenomenon of the 1980s. Butler and Wilson had brilliantly caught the mood of escapism, of post-feminist frivolity, and now they were ready to launch a range of outrageously tongue-in-cheek fantasy jewels, larger than life and frankly fake, echoing with the seductive glamour of Hollywood.

Over the years Butler and Wilson had also kept for their collection some examples of vintage American costume jewellery from the heyday of the industry. The American costume jewellery industry had blossomed in the 1930s at a time when the luxury goods trade was suffering from the economic crisis that followed the Wall Street Crash, and continued to flourish for twenty years. There was a need for escapism and diversion and for fashions that promised more dash for less cash.

The 1940s and '50s costume jewels collected by Butler and Wilson were pure fantasy jewels that expressed the impossible glamour of the movie stars and the aspirations and dreams of the stories they acted out on the silver screen. They chose pieces that were in no way imitations of the real thing, but instead made the most of the freedom offered by the materials, colours and techniques of fake jewellery. This Hollywood section of the collection includes a dazzling bib necklace from the late 1940s, of mixed diamanté and deep turquoise paste stones, the beautifully curved collar hung with a huge drop-shaped motif, and fringed with sparkling drop-shaped stones. This inspired a successful 1980s version, as did the massive 1940s all-diamanté collar with a tie. This was not jewellery for the faint-hearted, but for the flamboyant, self-confident woman of the 1940s, who followed the *garçonne* of the 1930s into an era of intense new femininity. Today's versions of these ultra-glamorous jewels also reflect and appeal to the new self-confident femininity of the present post-feminist age.

Joan Collins wearing Butler & Wilson, rejoices in Hollywood style.

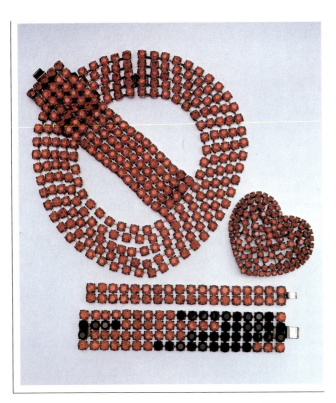

Butler and Wilson revive aristocratic glamour with dazzling diamanté versions of eighteenth-century bow brooches.

Previous pages: Two original 1950s necklaces in the Butler & Wilson collection, from the golden years of costume jewellery and the heyday of Hollywood glamour. Tie necklace in massive diamanté, a classic inspiration for a monumental mid-1980s accessory, c.1950.

BUTLER & WILSON ORIGINALS

Although inspired by earlier jewels and by the fashions and fabulous women of past eras, Butler & Wilson originals were totally modern, very much in tune with, or ahead of current fashions. It is their ability to follow their instincts and to keep one foot in history and the other in today's world that has accounted for so much of the success of their jewellery.

Butler and Wilson introduced the excitement of diamanté and fake pearls into more conventional designs, chokers and small earrings, twisted ribbed bracelets in two-coloured gilt metal, so that women became accustomed to the sparkling possibilities that glamour jewels could lend to their clothes and personalities. They progressed to the huge, bold and witty models that have become their trademark: 'Rhinestones as big as the Ritz', wrote the *Observer* at Christmas 1982.

Another reason for the surge of popularity of paste at this time was the return of black for evening. The little black dress had never been tinier. Minimalism held sway over fashion, lines became simpler, uncluttered, severe, and tight plain black dresses cried out for gleaming ornaments. Severity inspired a revival of grand costume jewellery. It also provided the perfect backdrop for many Butler & Wilson's creations.

The production of Butler & Wilson jewels, all made in British factories, now became more sophisticated and the quality of manufacture and materials and particularly of the gemstones was of vital importance. Model making and production techniques became gradually more and more refined to achieve the right effect for the new,

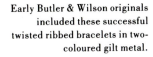

Early Butler & Wilson originals included these successful twisted ribbed bracelets in two-coloured gilt metal.

82

BUTLER & WILSON ORIGINALS

Gradually more and more diamanté was introduced to dramatic designs: the wing motif borrowed from the late nineteenth-century (*top left*); the graphic chequerboard earrings, inspired by the mid-1920s black and white vogue and impressive diamanté flowers (*below right*) echo the royal jewels.

Right: Jewels for the New Romantics of the early 1980s: courtly pastiches of eighteenth-century grandeur epitomized by the bow brooch, with the occasional Art Deco version in which the bow is hung on a circle (*far right*), and some elegant Edwardian variations.

exciting and ambitious designs. All the Butler & Wilson jewellery has always been set with stones from the Austrian firm Swarovski, who daily produce some 60 million of the world's finest quality crystal gemstones, of all colours, shapes, cuts and sizes.

Meanwhile, the beautiful blushing Princess of Wales was at the centre of the New Romanticism of the 1980s. She brought youth and glamour and high style to the Royal Family and the endless pictures of the new Princess at balls and official dinners inspired a pervasive fashion for ballgowns for the young: bare shouldered, tight bodiced, balanced by full, sweeping skirts of gleaming taffeta. Grand jewellery was needed to complete the romantic courtly look and diamanté suited the mood perfectly. Butler & Wilson supplied the New Romantics with pastiches of eighteenth-century grandeur, huge diamanté ribbon bows, fringed necklaces, long drop 'girandole' or chandelier earrings of superb style and proportions, regal and feminine to make each girl in her ballgown feel like a princess.

Princess Diana, following in the footsteps of Princess Alexandra, the previous Princess of Wales, who was equally elegant and fashionable, launched a massive mania for pearls. For several seasons in the early 1980s the pearl choker reigned supreme over the jewellery world, inspiring endless costume jewellery versions. Butler and Wilson varied the look by mixing pearls with diamanté, with black glass, or gilt metal and introducing big baroque or blister pearls. At this time, costume jewellery became socially acceptable for all occasions, even for the grandest of balls, and at all times of the day.

In the early 1980s, under the influence of the new Princess of Wales, the pearl choker reigned supreme over the jewellery world. Butler and Wilson varied the look in many ways, in this case adding movement and sensuality to the traditional necklace.

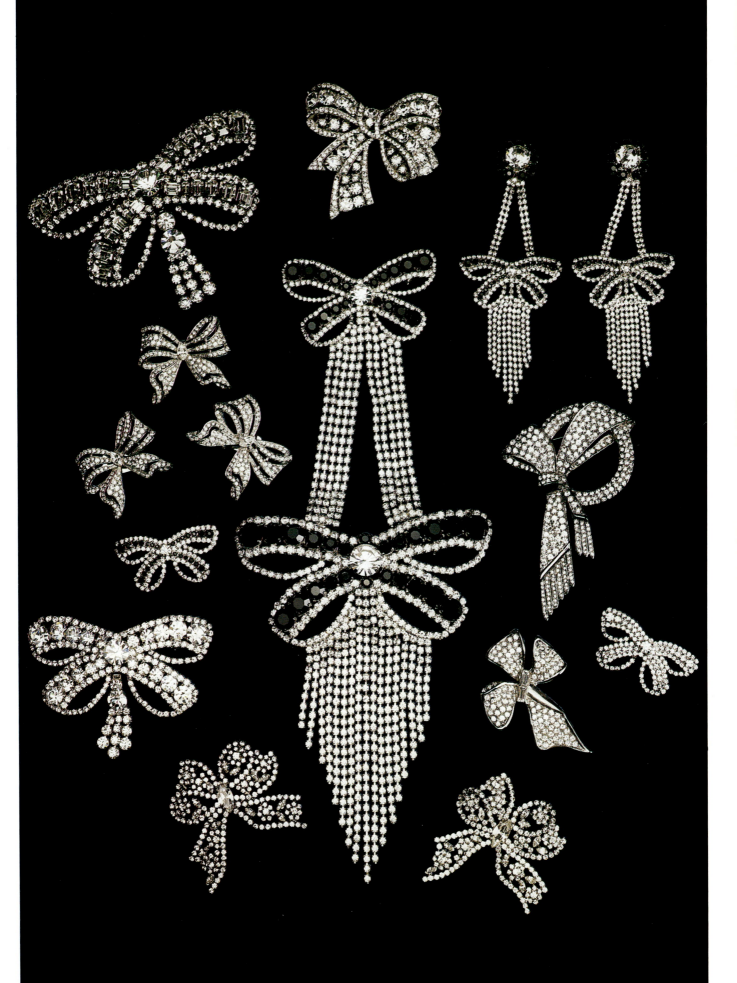

BUTLER & WILSON ORIGINALS

By 1984 the heavy metal look had arrived, an antidote to the sweetness of the New Romantics. In Paris Yves Saint Laurent and Azzedine Alaia had taken the bizarre costumes of the London street-pounding punk and converted them into an aggressive sexy look, typified by tight black clothes, studded black leather, little black boots. It was a strong look picked up by Butler and Wilson and assimilated into their fast-growing collection of daring and dazzling diamanté. In 1984 their new designs thrilled customers with a delicious metallic shock. As always the masters of the unexpected, Butler and Wilson mixed the biggest of diamanté with cool mechanical chains in steely tones of aluminium and pewter, producing cleverly engineered necklets, wide 'ton-up' wristbands, heavy chain bracelets in every width to be worn by the armful or one at a time. Romance was not completely dead: steel was studded with paste for heart-shaped earrings and necklaces, using varied textures and themes.

In 1984 Butler and Wilson were commissioned to make jewellery for the following year's Pirelli calendar, using the tyre-track motif. The mechanical theme fitted in perfectly with the prevailing heavy metal look. The zigzag pattern also conformed to Butler and Wilson's ideal of geometric modernist design, and they produced a series of diamanté and black glass ornaments based on or outlined as the tyre tread. The overall theme of the calendar was a fashion show, photographed by Norman Parkinson on location in Britain. All the clothes and accessories were designed by famous British fashion houses and designers, and each unique item featured the image of the Pirelli tyre tread. The Pirelli jewellery is now in the Victoria and Albert Museum.

Left: The heavy metal look of 1984 combined massive diamanté with the steely tones of aluminium and pewter-coloured metal.

Following pages: The Pirelli tyre-track jewellery of 1985; now in the Victoria and Albert Museum, London; the diamanté version (*left*), and (*right*) the steely, mechanical designs.

The overall theme for the Pirelli calendar of 1985 was a fashion show photographed by Norman Parkinson: Iman wears the Butler & Wilson jewellery with her tyre-track furs and the shops celebrate the Pirelli calendar event with special window displays in 1985.

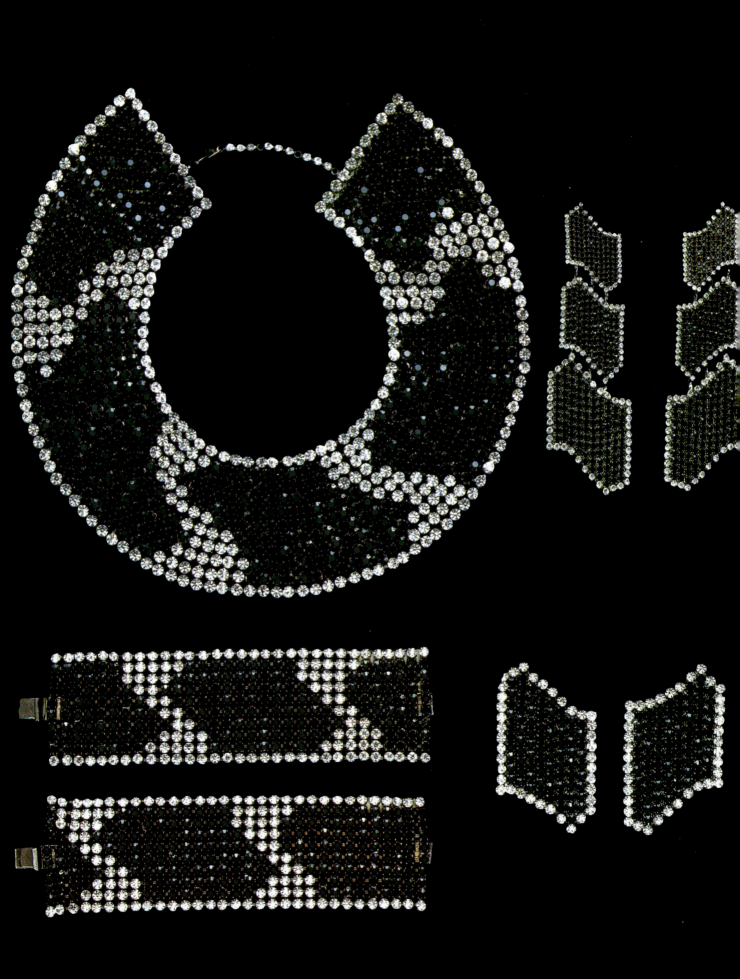

Butler & Wilson Originals

*T*he year of the 1984 Olympic Games became the year of the medal, of the young Olympian style. Medals offered an ideal way of adding colour and humour to austere, rather sombre clothes. The formal opulence of medals, orders and decorations had caught the attention of the two designers. They liked the associations of danger, patriotism and romance, the aristocratic splendour of the noble orders, the lavish decorations with sunbursts of diamonds or lashings of enamels, all hung on deeply coloured silk ribbons. Medals and orders are generally collected for their scarcity, their history and provenance, but Butler and Wilson now drew public attention to their classic and highly decorative beauty.

They used conventional shapes, the jagged sunburst in diamanté, circular badges with wreath and crown emblems, the Maltese cross, the crown, and in all a dramatic mixture of elements taken from many designs. Inspired by books of medals and decorations they juggled the proud conqueror's profile from Imperial Rome with the Russian eagles of Tsarist dynasties, and the Prince of Wales feathers. In this way Butler and Wilson brought all the drama and colour of military regalia, of British pomp and pageantry to high-fashion jewellery.

Right: These opulent medal jewels, in gilt metal, hung on rich silks proved a phenomenal world-wide success between 1984 and 1985.

1984, the year of the Olympic Games also became the year of the medal and Butler and Wilson's young Olympian look, modelled here by Nick Kamen. Twiggy (*right*) sports a variation on the noble theme with a crown and sword.

Butler & Wilson Originals

92

Huge brooches paved with diamanté were centred with a pale blue circle enclosing a red cross, creating an authentic impression and a rich and fashionable jewel. Plain gilt crosses were surmounted by an eagle, hung from grosgrain ribbons of purple, red, yellow or green, or centred with a white metal and enamelled motif and motto. There were well-modelled golden medallions paying homage to the Renaissance art of the medallist, and Maltese crosses surmounted with crossed swords or ribbons. Little lines of enamelled medals were hung with small crosses, crowns, and gilt emblems.

These glorious medals and orders caught the expert eye of Giorgio Armani, who promptly commissioned a special range to suit his own collection. Through Armani the craze spread yet more swiftly and further afield, and Butler and Wilson soon found that they had an extraordinary fashion phenomenon on their hands. Their medals expressed just the right look at the right time, and without doubt it was this medals story which took Butler and Wilson's reputation around the world. The fashion appealed to both men and women; Michael Jackson and Tina Turner flaunted their decorations; the connections with war and battle appealed to the punk contingent, while the rich and royal associations of medals, orders and decorations captured the imagination of the ultra-smart.

The craze for orders and decorations combined authentic colours and motifs with high fashion jewels: a matching set of diamanté, flashed with royal blue and red crosses; gilt medals and medallions ornamented with rich enamels, and a Maltese cross surmounted by an eagle.

Following pages: in the same spirit of opulence and tradition, Butler & Wilson charm bracelets, richly engraved and gem set.

BUTLER & WILSON ORIGINALS

Vogue saw the new charm bracelets as part of a classic English rose setting in 1984.

Right: Medals made of diamanté at the height of the fashion for glamour (*above*) and coin jewels, paying homage to the Renaissance art of the medallist, continued the parade of pageantry in the mid-1980s (*below*).

In this spirit of opulence and tradition, Butler and Wilson instigated a new fad for heavy golden charm bracelets, richly engraved and gem-set, recalling eighteenth- and early nineteenth-century seals and fobs of three-coloured gold with intricate chased rococo shells, scrolls and flowers, set with engraved gems. The same range was extended to include a lavish crown, orb, sceptre and swords, the symbols of the highest rank, deepest tradition and the ultimate, in jewellery terms, in history and pageantry. An eye-catching crown, richly gilt, was resplendent with a vibrant mixture of *faux* rubies, cornflower blue sapphires, diamonds and emeralds; golden orbs, also encircled with crystal gems, made superb earrings; miniature swords were ornamented with dashing gem-set hilts, and massive pendant crosses were also heavily gem-encrusted. This gallant heraldic story is a theme that has continued in more recent collections with the addition of the fleur-de-lys and a gilt metal suit of armour, diamanté fringing flowing from the helmet.

A lavish crown, resplendent with vibrant crystal stones, was another winning feature of this fashion; the ultimate in terms of historical jewels symbolizing rank and status.

Right: This gallant heraldic story continued into the late 1980s with motifs of the *fleur-de-lys*, shields, sword and a whimsical suit of armour with a flowing diamanté fringe.

The blackamoor ornamented with brilliant jewels and enamels has been a recurring theme in jewellery history, revived by Butler & Wilson, in gilt metal with *faux* turqoises, (*left*) or in their own individual style with riotously-coloured glass gems (*below*).

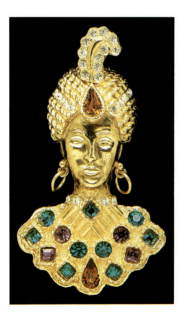

The blackamoor ornamented with brilliant jewels and enamels also fitted into the indulgent opulence of the mid 1980s. A recurring image in jewellery design, the blackamoor was found in eighteenth-century jewels and objects and then again in the late 1930s, with the craze for negro art, when Cartier created a series of exquisitely modelled clips of carved onyx, with gold, coral and turquoise, studded with precious stones. The beautiful trendsetting socialite Princess 'Baba' Faucigny Lucinge was the first to wear Cartier's jewelled blackamoors. Her close friend Diana Vreeland also wore them in rows and rows, mixing the fakes with the real thing. She couldn't tell the difference, she said, between the Cartier jewels and the copies sold by Saks at about $30 each. She wrote: 'I wore blackamoors the way Peggy Hopkins Joyce wore diamonds.' Butler and Wilson continued this tradition by creating jewels for the daring and avant-garde.

Butler & Wilson Originals

The ubiquitous serpent has wound its way through jewellery history from the ancient world, through the Victorians and Edwardians, to find yet another exalted position in twentieth-century costume jewellery in Butler & Wilson's designs of 1985 and '86. The meandering Victorian serpent, the Roman guardian spirit and symbol of eternity, was blown up larger than life, encrusted with diamanté and black glass and pearls so that it draped glistening around the neck or wound its way, one, two or three at a time over shoulder, bust or lapel.

Butler & Wilson's species possessed benign and beautiful qualities similar to those of their Victorian counterparts. In the nineteenth century, the serpent as a decorative device had connections both with the natural world and with antiquity. It became a favoured jewel emblem of the Romantics. Queen Victoria wore a serpent bracelet to her first council meeting and her betrothal ring took the form of a serpent set with emeralds. The early Victorian serpents with their flexible, scaly gold bodies and heavily gem-encrusted or enamelled heads, provided the leading inspiration for Butler and Wilson's mammoth models. Their long tapering bodies were also articulated, the heads shaped and stylized, with dramatic slanting eyes, a drop pearl representing the darting tongue.

The ubiquitous serpent (*right*) wound its way all through jewellery history to find a place in Butler and Wilson's menagerie, in diamanté, pearls and black glass beads. The slithering serpent became the fashion accessory of 1985 as confirmed in this photograph in *Vogue* (*above*).

Right: In 1986 jewelled lizards metamorphosed from restrained Edwardian ornaments into dazzling, oversized creatures in all sizes, styles and colours.

The most daring and successful of the family of lizards was this larger-than-life, articulated corsage ornament. As *Harpers & Queen* illustrated in 1986, these ravishing reptiles darted over the smartest figures for several seasons.

The Butler & Wilson menagerie expanded to include a family of penguins, ultra chic in black and white, enamelled and diamanté set, gilt metal bears, elephants and storks, and a brooch and earring set in the shape of a handsome parrot's head, with diamanté fringing.

In the early twentieth century, the lizard, the Roman symbol of wedded bliss, took over from the serpent to become the favourite animal motif in Edwardian jewellery, perhaps the most characteristic jewel emblem of that era. The lizard's little darting body and flicking tail were usually paved with diamonds, enriched with rubies or other gems, most characteristically and effectively set with a sinuous line of the grass green demantoid garnets which had been discovered towards the close of the previous century. This bright green suggested the colour of the creature but was also the favourite colour of Edward VII, who was particularly fond of peridots.

Butler and Wilson took the small and discreet Edwardian lizard brooch, and carefully maintaining its distinctive character, transformed it into a gigantic shimmering primeval creature, suggestive of prehistoric life, or of Eve, the first woman living in nature with such fantastic creatures clinging to her body. The Butler & Wilson lizard paved in diamanté had an inquisitive head, a curved body, a long lashing tail and little spread feet, that seemed to cling, pad-like, to a wide shoulder, a hip or the small of the back. Beautifully observed and re-scaled with fine proportions, the lizard offered all the magic, character and charm of classic historical jewels in the more modern

The lovable teddy bear proved to be a huge hit with sophisticated women at the height of the craze for massive diamanté novelties.

guise of wild fantasy. The lizards were made in a variety of colourways and materials, the most successful in diamanté with black glass, and they came in all sizes from petite to the enormously popular and outrageously oversized version, articulated and intended to crawl over the shoulder. The lizard, perhaps even more than the serpent, was turned into a massive fashion phenomenon.

With these highly successful creatures Butler and Wilson opened a whole menagerie of animals, birds and insects, all conceived with the same combination of sophistication with wit and humour. It was their deep understanding and appreciation of period jewellery that allowed them to break the rules. In the following years, Butler & Wilson's animal world came alive with floating Art Nouveau dragonflies, their favourite bugs from the 1930s recreated in diamanté, elephants' heads, beautifully modelled with long trunks and flapping ears, exotic parrots with long diamanté fringes, Scottie dogs modelled on 1930s lines, some with wagging heads, the ever-lovable Buster the Teddy bear, the gigantic spider with arched legs that sat menacingly on the shoulder. Traditionally women love to wear as jewels, and thus subdue, the creatures that most terrify them.

Butler and Wilson looked back to the 1930s for their most stylish dogs, several were made with nodding heads. The lady pulled by her dog was one of the most evocative of Art Deco images.

The gigantic diamanté spider was made to sit menacingly on the shoulder; a realistically modelled elephant's head with articulated trunk, all paved in diamanté; and a playful monkey swings from his branch, alongside an elephant with his trunk raised and a proud horse's head.

The Duchess of Windsor, a fashion leader of the 1930s and '40s, had always been an important influence on Butler and Wilson; their billboard showed a new way to flaunt Wallis's winning style.

The Duchess of Windsor, a fashion leader of the 1930s and '40s with an overwhelming passion and flair for jewel-wearing, has always been an important influence on Butler and Wilson. In April 1987 the extraordinary sale of the Duchess of Windsor's jewels at Sotheby's in Geneva added impetus to the growing trend towards glamour jewellery. The auction was the most spectacular jewellery event of the century and the jewels were seen not only as precious treasures, but also as the deeply personal mementoes of the love story that changed history.

The best of the jewels had been made in the late 1930s, the '40s and '50s, many of them by the great jewellers of the Place Vendôme. The highlights were the avant-garde, racy jewels of superb quality and powerful, adventurous design, custom-made for the Duchess by Cartier and Van Cleef & Arpels, the Windsors' favourite jewellers. So rich and extravagant were the designs and the use of gems that at first, acquaintances believed Mrs Simpson's jewels must be costume jewels. The Duchess of Windsor wore her jewels with great ease and panache, with the same daring irreverence that characterized their design.

The 'Big Cat' jewels and the flamingo brooch were the most exciting pieces in the collection and the most widely publicized. The diamond-set panthers, the prowling, sensual, jewelled wild animals, brilliantly articulated, tactile and supple, were the most closely associated with the Duchess's inimitable style. The panther was the symbol of sleek but predatory femininity, the sign of the *femme fatale*, and the Cartier jewels soon became the badges of the richest, most powerful women of the period including Barbara Hutton and the Princess Aga Khan. The impact of the jewels was due to the talent of Jeanne Toussaint, Cartier's chief designer whose own nickname was '*panthère*'.

The fabulous flamingo was also part of Toussaint's menagerie. Made in 1940 especially for the Duchess, the finely modelled bird with its plump diamond-set body perched on one spindly leg and its riotously coloured tail feathers epitomized the daring design of precious jewels and reflected the dazzling, determined femininity of the 1940s.

After the sale the costume jewellery industry feverishly turned out copies or pastiches, and Butler and Wilson produced an extravagant group of Wallis-inspired jewellery including an excellent version of the flamingo, and several well-observed variations on the big cat and panther theme, a fashion that was to last for several seasons.

The sale of the Duchess of Windsor's jewels had confirmed new interest in jewels of figurative fantasy and artistry, colour and glamour. Over the next few years Butler and Wilson introduced more

Butler and Wilson came up with a stunning collection inspired by the Duchess and the sale of the Windsor jewels featuring their versions of the famous flamingo and the 'Big Cat' jewels.

zany figurative forms, acutely observed cartoon characters; the jolly snowman for Christmas; skiers and reindeers for the winter; and for hotter days, returning to their infatuation with the Wild West, a most endearing lasso-swinging cowboy and a Mexican bandito, slouched dozing in the desert sun against a cactus.

For spring 1988, Butler and Wilson changed course and looked back to the sophistication of Art Deco and the glorious Grand Hotel years of stylish travel. This was a collection that reflected their fascination with Hollywood and the movies. Brooches were based on original 1920s designs of a pilot wearing goggles and flying hat, a stately ocean liner coasting alongside the New York skyline, cubist bellhops, buckled suitcases covered in evocative place names, entwined tango dancers. The same celebratory atmosphere of frenetic excitement was summoned up by a massive diamanté champagne glass spraying bubbles, while the travel theme moved on to another dimension with simple sculptural jewellery shaped as planets and stars.

In sharp contrast to the frankly fake and fabulously flippant diamanté fashions of the 1980s, Butler and Wilson also designed a range of ultra-modern sterling silver and gold-plated jewellery. These jewels cater to a different taste, and designs are based on simple sleek architectural lines, streamlined and mechanistic, with a textured matt surface. Shapes, forms and proportions have been drawn from their knowledge of modernist jewels, which so often anticipated the coming space age, but this range also shows their commitment to ultra-modern forward-looking late twentieth-century design.

In the late 1980s there were signs that a more tailored Chanel-inspired look was gaining ground from the huge and humorous diamanté. Butler and Wilson encouraged this shift of emphasis by creating an entirely new and alternative look, based on large creamy baroque pearls set in burnished gilt metal with a definite 'antique' finish. The 1989 collection expanded this theme and looked to the *fin de siècle*: it emerged as an opulent offering reminiscent of Byzantine splendour. Sensual and barbaric jewels featured wide slave bangles of antique gold, studded with silky pearls, ornamented with heavy twisted wirework, while the same antique gold was embedded with crystal gems of deep, rich jewel-like colours to create a new baroque sophistication for the 1990s, gloriously suggestive of turn-of-the-century decadence.

A favourite theme of 1988 was the Grand Hotel look, recalling the 1920s and '30s and an era of luxurious travel, recreated by bellhops and dancing waiters, little cubist figures or lively characters in lavish diamanté with flexible legs fringes to add to the impression of movement.

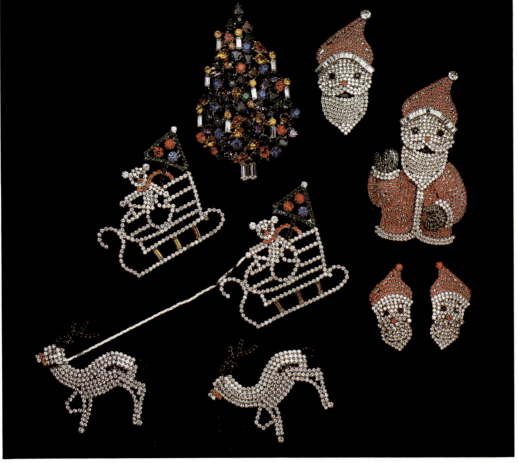

Some of the most popular Butler & Wilson novelties: enamelled movie-style telephone jewels; twinkling Christmas fantasies and the spectacular champagne cocktail brooch, bubbling with nostalgia, glamour and diamanté.

Butler & Wilson Originals

At the close of the 1980s, Butler and Wilson introduced a new, rich Baroque style of patinated gilt metal encrusted with soft pearls or rich *faux* gems.

As an alternative to diamanté and fantasy jewels, Butler and Wilson have created a range of sleek, mechanistic and architectural silver and silver gilt jewellery, its style captured by Patrick Demarchelier for *Vogue* 1990 (*above/right*).

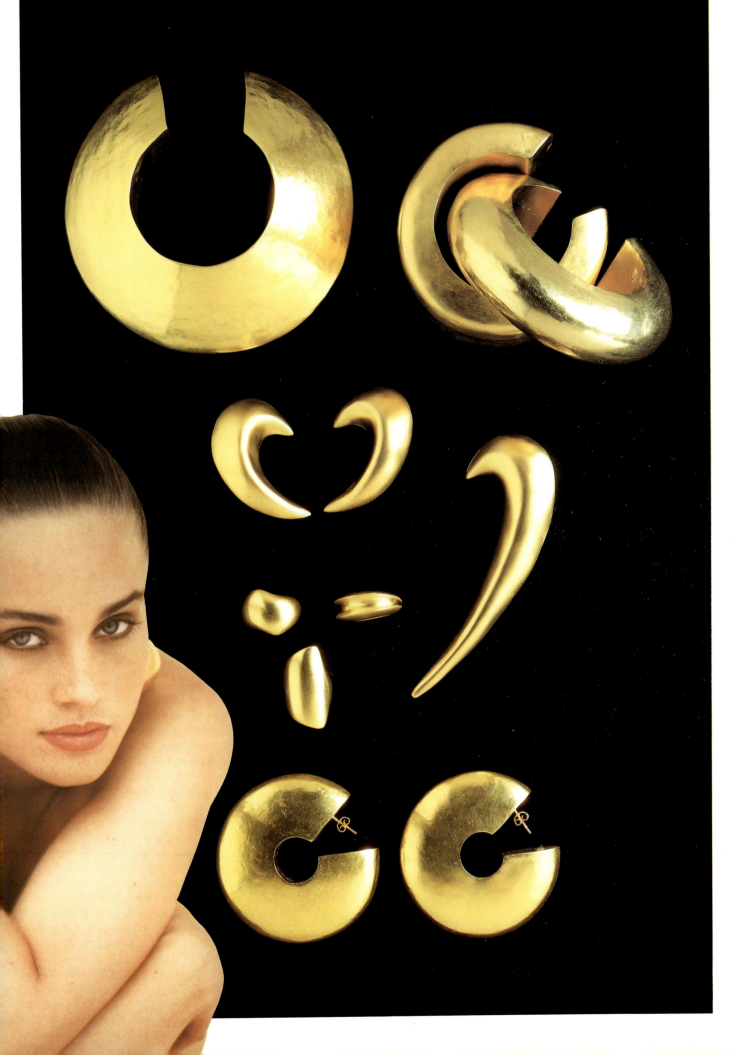

Part Two

CREATING THE IMAGE

Butler and Wilson's stylish and personal approach to jewellery has always attracted a glamorous, star-studded clientele. In their early days, their stand in Antiquarius was a regular haunt for ultra-fashionable women, including many of the most famous models of the day. At that time models were celebrities and they married rock stars like Roger Daltry and Eric Clapton, who also came shopping for antique accessories. Actors and actresses came too, and a variety of other stylish personalities, Jane Fonda and Roger Vadim, Bianca Jagger, Julie Christie, the spectacular model Veruschka, Celia Birtwell and Ossie Clarke. Barbara Hulanicki, the founder of Biba, was one of Butler & Wilson's best customers. Linda McCartney bought her husband's wedding ring there: a flexible gold chain ring set with a heart-shaped green stone.

Men and women involved with establishing a new culture, whether in clothes or music, in photography, the cinema or journalism, were all drawn to London's bizarre and buzzing antiques markets with their intriguing relics of past lives, cultures and crazes, and Butler & Wilson's stand became the favourite place for 'alternative' jewellery and accessories.

The new breed of fashion editors also gravitated towards Antiquarius and their directional editorial shots accessorized with Butler & Wilson

Above: This 1970s model wears a huge, ultra-modern gilt and black necklace.

Left: Bianca Jagger decorated with classic Butler & Wilson jewels, the ever popular cicada brooches, photographed for *Cosmopolitan* in 1972.

period pieces exerted a particularly strong influence on readers. Yet more women turned up at the stand wanting to look just like the models. Some of the most successful shots styled by *Vogue* fashion editor Grace Coddington featured the beautiful young model Ingrid Boulting, 'the Biba girl', photographed by Barry Lategan wearing soft mellow, mustard colours, flattered by stylish Art Deco jewellery, and armfuls of plastic bangles in similar muted tones.

Fabulous and famous women, particularly those icons of the 1920s and '30s, had always inspired Butler and Wilson: from the time they first started selling jewellery they took a keen interest in the way women looked, and in the way women could use fashions, accessories and jewels to play up their individuality. Several of the style leaders of the twentieth century who had captured their imagination had also helped to shape their tastes and inspire their milestone photographs of beautiful women.

They had long admired the sleek simplicity of the Duchess of Windsor, the chic ingenuity of Diana Vreeland, the sensational Josephine Baker, the witty Elsa Schiaparelli, the society siren Nancy Cunard, and the bejewelled eccentric Edith Sitwell. They took an interest in Edith Head and the splendour of her costume designs for the movies in the 1940s and '50s that epitomized the spirit of Hollywood glamour, and were fascinated by the polished sophistication of American socialite and jewel-collector Millicent Rogers. All of these women, although not conventional beauties, created a powerful personal style of their own, and all wore their jewels, both real and costume jewels, with exceptional flair.

Josephine Baker, the black American dancer from the ghettos of St Louis, became the rage of Paris in 1925 when she appeared half-naked at the Théâtre des Champs Elysées. She was nineteen and had come to Paris with a group of black entertainers to take part in a song and dance show called the Revue Nègre, aimed at making the most of the prevailing craze for Negro art and culture and all things African. Her comic dance routines had caused a sensation on Broadway and now Josephine Baker took Paris by storm. This dusky-skinned girl, with her explosive uninhibited energy and her superb body that contorted like rubber, came to embody the spirit of Paris in the 1920s.

As the organizers of the Revue Nègre wanted to present a vision of the archetypal African native, Baker was persuaded to appear bare-breasted and wearing nothing but feathers, the first of many outrageous costumes which became her hallmark and the talk of the town. She is best remembered for the little skirt of bananas worn for

Ingrid Boulting photographed by Barry Lategan for *Vogue* in the early 1970s, wearing armfuls of Art Deco bakelite bangles and rows of semi-precious beads.

Josephine Baker exudes the energy and mad exuberance that set Paris alight in the 1930s.

The wild and wilful Nancy Cunard photographed by Cecil Beaton wearing her famous ivory African fighting bangles.

her savage but joyful dance performed at the *Folies Bergère*, but on other occasions her body glimmered with diamanté. Off-stage, she loved couture clothes, especially the latest models from Poiret. Within a year she had stirred up a mad craze among chic Paris fashion followers. They rubbed walnut oil on their skin to darken it, slicked down their hair, pinned little curls around the forehead and wore dramatic, glittering jazz age clothes.

For 1920s sophisticated drama and memorable jewel-wearing, the image of **Nancy Cunard**, the daughter of the fabled Emerald, Lady Cunard, must remain unrivalled. In a very different way she too expressed the pulsating African influence that was to contribute so much to twentieth-century art and design. The Colonial Exhibition of 1922 had revealed to Europe sensational African artefacts, ornaments and jewels, and it was probably Nancy Cunard who did most to popularize the vogue for barbaric jewellery. She brought an aroma of wild savagery to the London social scene, where she was famed for her armfuls of ivory bangles, genuine African fighting bangles, used originally in tribal warfare. Occasionally their new owner, in a similarly hostile mood, found them immensely useful for throwing at her long-suffering friends.

The bangles were of varying widths and shapes, some wide like scooped-out bone, others smooth and rounded rings, always worn row upon row up to the elbow. She posed with these ritualistic body ornaments for photographs by Cecil Beaton in the late 1920s, her hair scraped back, in a tight fitting cap, her wild wide eyes rimmed and smudged with kohl. 'Her fine-boned arms were encased in such a concatenation of weighty armlets of rigid African ivory that the least movement produced a clacking sound of billiard balls or the cakewalk of a skeleton,' wrote Daphne Field in her book on the Cunards.

Perhaps more than any other woman at the time, the legendary couturier **Gabrielle 'Coco' Chanel** stamped her own forceful style on this period and brought fashion and jewels closer together. In the process she totally overturned attitudes towards costume jewellery. She had had an austere upbringing from the age of twelve as an orphan in a spartan convent in France. Perhaps it was this deprivation in the midst of the lavish Belle Epoque that drove her to strive for success; later, her famous fakes were parodies of the fabulous, enormously valuable jewels worn by the aristocrats and courtesans of her youth.

Starting as a humble seamstress she made her way to become the most successful couturier of her day, and probably the most famous name in twentieth-century fashion. She instigated a fashion for simple jersey clothes, shirtdresses, sailor suits, cardigans, all with shorter skirts and in loose easy fabrics for maximum freedom of movement, to let the body and character shine through. Her relaxed style was known as *poverty de luxe*. She soon became a trendsetter herself, and when she cut her hair in 1917 it caused a sensation and launched a worldwide fashion for the 'bob'. She dressed up her simple clothes with piles of unashamedly fake jewels, yards of impossibly large and lustrous pearls worn incongruously with her casual cardigans and sweater dresses. She taught women to wear jewellery on all occasions, at all times of day, turning the rules of jewel-wearing on their head.

The grandeur of heavily brocaded English livery uniforms inspired her to produce sumptuous baroque gilt jewels, chains and medallions, and she recreated magnificent gemstones in handmade coloured glass to invoke a magical Byzantine richness. Chanel wore her own jewels, some real, some non-precious or semi-precious, with memorable chic:

Veiled and bejewelled, the legendary Coco Chanel.

she was especially fond of a pair of enamelled bangles encrusted with gem-set Maltese crosses, designed by the Duke of Verdura, who created Chanel's costume jewellery in the 1920s and '30s. She was much photographed wearing these bangles, along with a great deal of costume jewellery.

It was her fierce rivalry with Schiaparelli that drove her to create an ever stronger image of herself, and she surrounded herself with a golden gathering of world-renowned photographers, including Horst, Hoyningen-Huené, Cecil Beaton and later Avedon, who each in his highly individual manner immortalized Chanel's inimitable style, sharp yet casual, the epitome of the modern woman.

Elsa Schiaparelli was Chanel's arch rival: Chanel brought grandeur and respectability to costume jewels; Schiaparelli gave them magic and fantasy. Schiaparelli was a brilliant innovator; her zany wit, expressed in her designs for clothes and jewels, summed up the creative madness and frenetic freedom of Paris between the wars.

A champion of surrealism, she loathed the ordinary and the banal, and one of her first innovations was to turn buttons and fastenings into major jewel-like features of her clothes. Next she turned her jewels into surreal *objets d'art*, like the floating highly coloured elements of a dream. She always came up with the unexpected, but she had an innate sense of just how far to go, how far to take the joke. Tailored suits were fixed with buttons shaped as acrobats or bugs, or fruit and vegetables; an ultra-feminine white organza gown was splashed with a Dali-inspired boiled red lobster.

Butler and Wilson have always enjoyed this juxtaposition of the incongruous, Schiap's transformation of everyday subjects into fantasy jewels. She drew inspiration from the peculiarities of nature, from life around her, her extensive travels, and from myths and fairy tales. Her jewels were shaped as coffee beans, spinning tops, padlocks, vegetables, mermaids, ostriches, seaweed. The most successful and whimsical of her couture jewels were made by Jean Schlumberger, the young designer from Alsace whose talent was spotted and harnessed by Schiaparelli in the 1930s. Her courage and vitality encouraged his lively imagination and their short but fruitful collaboration produced some of the most extraordinary fantasy jewels of the period.

Schiaparelli possessed immense charisma and a personal style that emphasized her unconventional but dramatic looks. She loved wearing jewels, real and costume jewellery; her own real jewels, many of which came from the Paris jeweller Herz, were also avant-garde, usually based on surreal or organic motifs. Wearing her own mad hats, tailored clothes and magical jewels, her faraway spirit was captured by photographers including Horst, De Meyer and Irving Penn.

Schiaparelli's brilliant blend of wit and discipline contributed a great deal to the polished elegance of the Duchess of Windsor, who bought seventeen outfits from Schiaparelli's Music Collection of 1937 for her trousseau. The Duchess developed a deceptively simple style, accessorized by jewels created with daring imagination and worn with verve and a certain disregard for the heirloom syndrome. Her jewels were at once both precious yet whimsical and modern in design. It was the ease with which she wore her jewels, the balance between her severe and superbly cut clothes and her adventurous and luxurious jewellery that caught Butler and Wilson's imagination. They had always enjoyed the many evocative photographs of the Duchess, the romantic portraits by Beaton, the icy elegance captured by Horst, and

by Hoyningen-Huené, pictures that came to represent the style and atmosphere of an era and a story that changed the course of history.

Diana Vreeland, legendary magazine editor, was *the* fashion arbiter of the twentieth century. French-born, she inherited a sharp sense of style and fashion, form and colour, and became fashion editor of *Harper's Bazaar* in 1939. After twenty-five years she left to become editor-in-chief of *Vogue*, where she stayed until 1971, when she began work as consultant to the Costume Institute of the Metropolitan Museum in New York. It was her flamboyant personality and her celebrated taste, always decisively and readily expressed, that inspired so many designers, editors, photographers and models.

Diana Vreeland loved jewels: she revelled in their drama and fantasy, and for her they were always an essential part of fashion. She

Elsa Schiaparelli, whose brilliant blend of zany wit and discipline in both fashion and jewellery have had a strong influence on Butler & Wilson designs.

cared only for style and had no prejudices about value, although she appreciated rich gemstones and the dramatic gesture of an outrageously precious jewel worn with great panache. She wore both real and fake jewellery, often mixing them successfully, as with her rows and rows of blackamoors. She cherished innovative design, but loved the richness of medieval traditions and the splendour of Renaissance motifs, redolent with chivalry, heraldry and above all romance. Diana Vreeland had befriended and encouraged both Schlumberger and Verdura at the start of their careers, as costume jewellery designers to

Diana Vreeland who understood and appreciated jewels, both precious and non-precious, developed an inimitable personal style and influenced several generations of fashion magazines.

Schiaparelli and Chanel respectively, and she followed them both as they moved into the world of real jewellery.

Millicent Rogers was Diana Vreeland's lifelong friend, and together they shared a passion for jewels. The heiress to the Standard Oil fortune, Millicent Rogers married three times, had a well-publicized affair with Clark Gable, and was a great collector and celebrated socialite. Above all she was remembered for her superb dress sense, and for her fabulous jewels. Millicent Rogers epitomized expensive American society elegance of the 1940s. Her most

Millicent Rogers, American socialite and jewel collector, photographed wearing a sophisticated mixture of opulent medals and rugged turquoise and silver American Indian jewellery.

exquisite, sculptured gowns came from English-born New York couturier Charles James, while her jewellery collection included pieces by Cartier, Chaumet, and Schlumberger, although after World War II when she moved to Taos, New Mexico she fell in love with American Indian and Navajo jewellery.

She wore armfuls of massive silver and turquoise bracelets, '20s-style, mixed unexpectedly with a huge jewelled order or medal, the brutality of the Navajo ornaments set off to perfection by her sleek, well-bred sophistication. It was particularly her extensive collection

CREATING THE IMAGE

of Navajo jewels, (now in the Millicent Rogers Museum, Taos) and the way in which she wore them, that impressed Butler and Wilson, inspired their American Indian revival of the early '80s and encouraged their own ideas of combining unexpected jewellery styles.

Keeping in mind these favourite visions of charismatic women, Butler and Wilson set out to encourage individuality and femininity in the 1980s and to show women how to wear jewellery and use it to express their personalities. They gradually enticed many celebrated and glamorous clients to enjoy their jewels, to use their imagination when mixing fashion and costume jewellery and above all to wear it with pride and a sense of fantasy and freedom.

The ultimate demonstration of this new attitude has been given by the **Princess of Wales**, the supreme fashion leader of our time and probably the most photographed woman in the world. When she was seen in public on official occasions wearing Butler & Wilson, the highest social seal of approval was set on costume jewellery. Both the Princess of Wales and the Duchess of York are known to treasure their diamanté and are regular visitors to the Fulham Road shop.

The Princess of Wales wearing bow and heart drop earrings (*above*), and showing style when she pinned a snake brooch on the jacket of her tuxedo suit at a rock concert (*right*).

The Princess of Wales started by wearing their discreet and romantic silver and crystal heart and bow earrings which went on to become famous best-sellers, and then she gradually moved on to bolder, tongue-in-cheek designs which have acted as a barometer of her growing self confidence and her own developing fashion sense. She cleverly uses the jewellery to add a strong touch of individuality to couture clothes.

In May 1986 she caused a fashion sensation when she appeared in a black tuxedo suit with a white ruffled shirt for a rock concert during Expo'86 in Vancouver, Canada. This time it was her own dinner suit by Jasper Conran, and not one she had borrowed from her husband, but the most talked-about element in the outfit was the jewellery she chose. It was a slithering diamanté and black glass serpent brooch, the latest in Butler & Wilson's reptilian range. The Princess went on to choose some of the most unashamedly fake models: a diamanté teddy bear, a bejewelled cross with a strong medieval, ecclesiastical flavour, and for a film premiere she pinned a star-shaped enamelled and diamanté medal on a dramatic black and red Murray Arbeid evening gown.

The Duchess of York also enjoys her costume jewellery but tends to opt more for humorous designs, such as a sporting diamanté tennis racket, or the array of sparkling British and American flags worn in her hair on an official visit to Los Angeles in spring 1988.

THE BILLBOARDS
1982-1990

*I*n 1982 Butler and Wilson embarked on a series of billboard photographs in the tradition of the great portraits and publicity stills of the Hollywood legends: beautiful women portrayed by the world's most talented photographers. They took over a prominent billboard site, outside the Fulham Road shop, and every two months they presented a startling new image, which was often witty, sexy and daring, but always dignified and supremely stylish.

By this time, Butler and Wilson had collected glamorous clientele of famous, beautiful women, who could all well afford the real thing but enjoyed the excitement of ingenious costume jewellery. Butler and Wilson had designed jewels for Catherine Deneuve in the film *The Hunger*, and they asked if she would agree to become the first of the illustrious billboard legends. She was photographed by David Bailey, wearing classic low-key pearls. Catherine Deneuve recalls that the billboard photograph was mutually satisfying, as she has always admired Butler and Wilson's approach to jewellery. At the time she was attracted by their Victorian Scottish jewellery, which she has collected ever since, and now she loves their fantasy jewellery. 'It's glamorous but never pretentious; it's extreme but never pretends to be real. I very often mix real and fake jewellery. Dressing and wearing jewellery should be fun and fantasy jewels are fun. They also say something important about the wearer. Only people who are aware of real jewellery can truly appreciate fake jewellery.'

Deneuve was followed shortly by Charlotte Rampling and Faye Dunaway, both dedicated customers. Faye Dunaway was photographed by her husband Terry O'Neill, supremely relaxed and wearing armfuls of bangles, inspired by 1920s classics but resolutely up to date. Faye Dunaway wore an enormous diamanté hand brooch in another of O'Neill's photographs, its blend of serenity and surrealism echoing the great fashion photographs of the 1920s and '30s.

These women headed a glittering cast of famous beauties, models, actresses and celebrities including Marie Helvin, Lauren Hutton,

Shakira Caine, Charlotte Lewis, Jerry Hall, Twiggy, Sophie Ward, Marisa Berenson, Talisa Soto, Ali MacGraw and the megastar Dame Edna Everidge, well plastered in paste, as well as some decorative men, including Little Richard and Nick Kamen.

The world's best photographers were commissioned to do justice to these subjects and to create enduring images capturing the essence of the woman and her style. Terry O'Neill's women were modern intelligent romantics, Robert Mapplethorpe imposed a brutal beauty, Bailey's interpretations were graphic, powerful fashion classics and Helmut Newton's shots sizzled with dramatic sexuality. Butler and Wilson also explored the talents of John Swannell, Jamie Morgan, Norman Parkinson and Barry Lategan, who had originally taken quintessential jewellery photographs for *Vogue* in the late 1960s.

To demonstrate the witty intelligent woman of the 1980s, successfully combining independence and femininity, Butler and Wilson chose television journalist and presenter Sue Lawley for a 1988 billboard. Sue Lawley has been a Butler & Wilson customer for many years and she explained that for her their jewels are often more appealing than the real thing.

'I used to wear very discreet brooches, and Butler & Wilson's antique pieces were better for reading the news. Now I enjoy wearing their larger-than-life jewels on television as I need to project that bit more. Occasionally I also like to make a small visual joke, as I did wearing the giant lizard or the bubbly champagne glass.

'Their jewellery makes you feel good, light-hearted and fun, and it puts a sparkle in your eyes. People react well to it and you can wear it without being defensive. It is totally mentionable and as an icebreaker it is more interesting than the weather.'

Butler and Wilson's jewels with their long and rich ancestry in the history of design, together with the vibrant new image they have created for women, have allowed women their greatest expression of individuality in fashion for many decades. In their twenty-one years of business, they have managed to break down social barriers and overturn established rules of jewel-wearing in order to herald a brilliant new age of adornment.

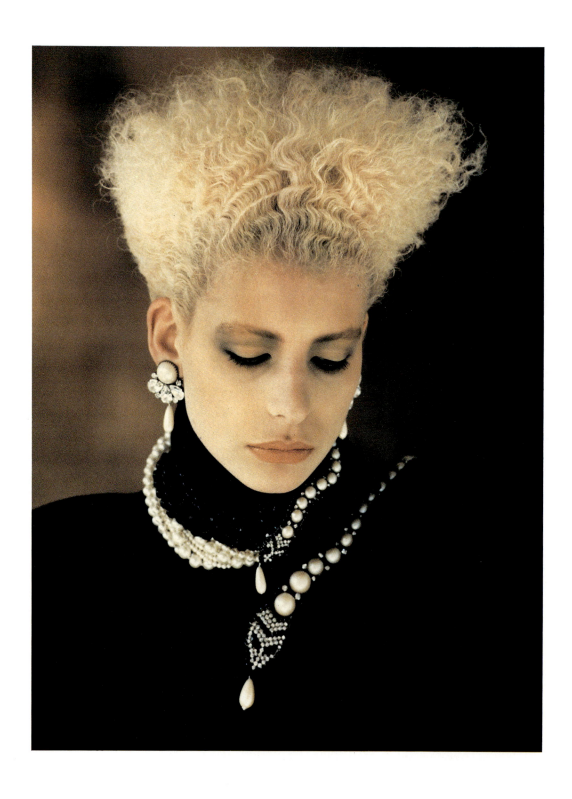

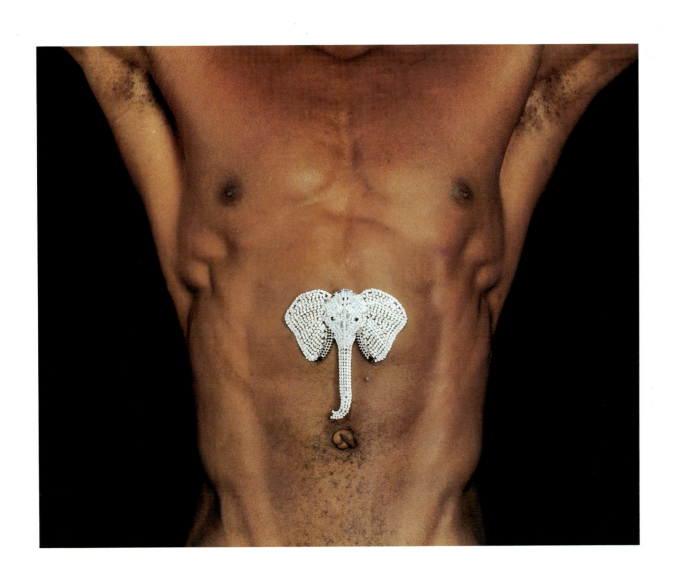

The Billboards
Models and Photographers

CATHERINE DENEUVE
David Bailey, page 135

IMAN PIRELLI CALENDAR SHOT
Norman Parkinson, page 137
By courtesy of Vogue © The Condé Nast Publications Limited

CHARLOTTE RAMPLING
Helmut Newton, page 138

RACHEL WARD
Perry Ogden, page 139

JULIA MANCINI
Stefano Massimo, page 140

JILL GOODACRE
Neil Kirk, page 141

FAYE DUNAWAY
Terry O'Neill, pages 142/143

POSTER DESIGN
Sara Sturgeon, pages 144/145
Winner of R.C.A. Butler & Wilson Billboard Competition

TOKO
John Swannell, pages 146/147

MARIE HELVIN
David Bailey, pages 148/149

MIMI
Neil Kirk, page 150

MARIANNE SWANNELL
John Swannell, page 151

LAUREN HUTTON
Jamie Morgan, pages 152/153

DAME EDNA EVERIDGE
Terry O'Neill, page 154

LITTLE RICHARD
Terry O'Neill, page 155

CLIO GOLDSMITH
Stefano Massimo, page 156

CHARLOTTE LEWIS
Terry O'Neill, page 157

THOMAS
Robert Mapplethorpe, pages 158/159

SHAKIRA CAINE
Neil Kirk, page 160

TALISA SOTO
Norman Watson, page 161

SUE LAWLEY
Terry O'Neill, page 162

ALI MacGRAW
John Swannell, page 163

MADALENA
Stefano Massimo, page 164

MARPESSA
Marco Sacchi, page 165

FRENCH AND SAUNDERS
Trevor Leighton, pages 166/167

TANYA COLRIDGE
Helmut Newton, pages 168/169

TATJANA PATITZ
Marco Sacchi, pages 170/171

CATHERINE BAILEY
David Bailey, pages 172/173

ACKNOWLEDGEMENTS

Photographers
David Bailey 16
Cecil Beaton 125, 127, 129, 130
David Cochran 11
Louise Dahl-Wolfe 131
Patrick Demarchelier 118
Normal Eales 120
Tim Graham 133
Christian Hartann 84
Hoyningen-Heune 124
Steve Hiett 90
Peter Knapp 25
Eddy Kohli 73
Paul Lange 100
Barry Lategan 34, 53, 123
Trevor Leighton 176
Rudi Molacek 8
Perry Ogden 62, 67 (Sophie Ward)
Terry O'Neill 2 (Jerry Hall)
Alberto dell'Orto 68
Norman Parkinson 87
Harry Peccinotti 9
Mike Reinhardt 72
Steven Silverstein 103
John Swannell 13 (Marianne Swannell), 49 (Toko),
53 (Toko), 90, 110 (Marianne Swannell)
John Stember 81
Bruce Weber 96
All still-life photographs by
Tom Dawes and Prudence Cummings Associates
Special thanks to Terry O'Neill

Reproductions courtesy of:
Cosmopolitan 120
Harpers and Queen 8, 68
Harvard Theatre Collection 124
Observer Magazine, styled by Ann Boyd 121
Over 21 Magazine, model Sue Purdy 86
Sotheby's 125, 127, 129, 130
Vidal Sassoon 84, 96
Vogue, Condé Nast Publications Ltd 11, 16, 25, 34, 53,
60, 72, 81, 87, 100, 118, 123

Left to Right: Simon Wilson, Dawn French, Jennifer Saunders and Nicky Butler